GORILLA KILLER

A TRUE STORY OF BETRAYAL, BRUTALITY AND BUTCHERY

RYAN GREEN

For Helen, Harvey, Frankie and Dougie

Disclaimer

This book is about real people committing real crimes. The story has been constructed by facts but some of the scenes, dialogue and characters have been fictionalised.

Polite Note to the Reader

This book is written in British English except where fidelity to other languages or accents are appropriate. Some words and phrases may differ from US English.

YOUR FREE BOOK IS WAITING

From bestselling author Ryan Green

There is a man who is officially classed as "**Britain's most dangerous prisoner**"

The man's name is Robert Maudsley, and his crimes earned him the nickname "**Hannibal the Cannibal**"

This free book is an exploration of his story...

★★★★★ *"Ryan brings the horrifying details to life. I can't wait to read more by this author!"*

Get a free copy of ***Robert Maudsley: Hannibal the Cannibal*** when you sign up to join my Reader's Group.

www.ryangreenbooks.com/free-book

CONTENTS

All Men Are as Beasts in the Eyes of God

It was a rather pleasant afternoon in the receiving room of a charming boarding house. Sunshine shone in through the lace and traced delicately over the chintz.

The visitor was a black block amongst the florals. Stern and dark from the top of his slicked-back hair to the tips of his well-shined shoes. He kept his hat clasped between his hands as he spoke, taking his time to carefully enunciate each and every word - as if he was pondering over everything he said before he'd allow it to slip loose of his protruding lips. He was not a handsome man by any stretch of the imagination, brutish looking with his sloped brow, but it was his hands that the eye was drawn back to over and over. Hair had crept up the back of them, leaving bare-knuckles before sprouting on his fingers. Even that, though, was not the mortifying detail that kept the poor landlady fixedly staring at her coffee cup. The hands were as big as her head. Each one of them could have encompassed her entire face with ease. Freakshow prurience kept drawing her eyes back down the soberly dressed man, back to his hat and the fingers there - thick as a paper-packet of sausages from the good butcher.

Just to look at him, there was not a chance that an available room would be in the offing. Most of the clientele in this boarding house were widows, older ladies who needed a certain level of peace and quiet, or the complaints would start flowing. A man that size would surely have footsteps like thunder. A young man thundering up and down the stairs through the night would trouble everyone's sleep, and that was the type of man who sought out a boarding house rather than more permanent accommodations, was it not? A salesman passing through town had no good reason to be well-mannered when he'd never cross the paths of any he met again. This man had the look of an animal about him. What was to stop him behaving like an animal while he stayed under her roof?

Yet the softness of his voice began to beguile her. She would have expected a man so large to rumble in his chest with every word, but instead, the words came out pure and smooth. The first time that he quoted scripture in the conversation, it all came to an abrupt halt. She knew he was a salesman of sorts, but it was then that she began to suspect what he sold.

 He was not a prideful man by any stretch, and he seemed so bashful to talk about himself that she almost felt bad for prying, but it would not do to invite a strange man in amongst the ladies without some proper vigilance applied. For now, his softness was balancing the sight of those hands quite readily, but it still wasn't enough to tip things in his favour.

He handled the coffee cup awkwardly, the tiny china pieces moving beyond delicate and into cartoonish in his grasp. When he sipped from it, he did not slurp, but neither did he seem to take much pleasure in it, either.

Eventually, her suspicions about him were proven correct. Though he had the looks of an ape, there was a missionary's fire in his eyes and a sureness to him that was belied by his soft speech. He drew out a Bible from his jacket pocket and set it on his knee. This was his stock-in-trade. Not fripperies and gadgets, but the gospel truth. The good word in printed form, sold door to door among those places in even the Lord's own America where the ungodly had found footing. He expressed his admiration for those who travelled further afield, into the dangerous depths of the dark continent to bring the good word to the savage, but as he quite rightly said, there was nobody speaking to the savage on the doorstep in their own tongue.

She wondered if he might not have a little of the savage in him himself with that broad face and swarthy tan. There might have been some mulatto in that mix. Some ape-man having his way with a godly woman to create offspring like this, one that would turn heads as it lumbered down the street. The sins of the father were laid on the child, visiting iniquity upon the sons of the third and fourth generation. He might well have been a few generations down the tree from his jungle roots.

Still, as he mumbled to himself when she asked if that meant he had to enter dens of iniquity to spread the good word, 'Judge not lest ye be judged.' She herself was not without sin, and in denying him some safe place to retreat to after a hard day's work trying to sell his Bibles to the godless, wouldn't she be casting the first stone?

He was not working hard to convince her. That would have raised alarms in her mind all on its own. For a young man to be pushing at her to make a decision would have raised her hackles. Rather it was like he was a man of the law, standing in the court where she presided and presenting his case. Leaving it to her to decide whether his case was just or folly. She liked that. It flattered her ego for a man to so fully supplicate himself before her.

All the salesmen before came in with an attitude that rubbed her wrong. They assumed that the place was theirs. They assumed that this little old lady would just roll over the minute they raised their voices and pushed their luck.

A man the size of this Bible salesman could have blustered and pushed from the get-go and probably gotten his way by intimidation alone in most of the boarding houses about town, yet not once had he been so coarse. He had shown the utmost respect to her from the moment he answered her posted advertisement. Even as he'd come up the stairs to greet her and she'd taken in his bulk for the first time, he had done his very best to put her at ease, sloping his shoulders and leaning down so that he wouldn't loom over her. He was clearly a man aware of his affliction in the area of appearance and doing his very best to make the least of it that he could.

After so many years in this business, thick skin was a requirement. If he had attempted any tomfoolery with her, then he would have been out on his hide before they made it so far as the receiving room, but even now, with his case presented with all due diligence and politeness, the Bible salesman was just chatting away to her politely. He was uncomfortable, clearly ill at ease with small talk and frequently slipping back into his Biblical pronouncements when at a loss for words of his own, but the more time that she spent with him, the more at ease the landlady felt. As though his lack of confidence empowered her. This was not a man to come in at odd hours or to make odd demands. This was a good man. A godly man. One devoted to bending no grass blades beneath his steps and nudging nobody aside to reach his destination.

He did so well throughout his interview that the landlady was already set to shake his hand and welcome him in without even asking the final question. It was out of character of her to break from her routines, and even more out of character to make snap decisions. It wasn't as if the final question even had much bearing on the decision she'd make, but she pressed on to it nonetheless.

'What made you choose this boarding house?'

The question seemed to surprise him, as though it had never occurred to him that he might be asked. He chewed it over for a long moment before an answer finally crept out. 'I was raised in an old house, a godly one full of kindness, but an old one all the same. Since then, I've had a fondness for older places. The ones which show character instead of skin-deep beauty.' He looked around the room where they sat, fingers pinching the brim of his hat. 'Your decorations are modern, but the bones of the place show such promise. Just look up there at the plasterwork on that ceiling.'

The landlady looked up at her roof as if for the first time, taking in the mouldings around the walls and the medallion around the gas lamp chandelier. She couldn't help but smile. All it took was fresh eyes to see the beauty in all things. When she glanced back to her guest, she expected him to be staring up still at the unfamiliar rose pattern. Instead, his eyes remained fixed on her, and a grin had spread across his face - one that he allowed to fade back to a friendly smile when his eyes drifted back up from her neck to her face.

For an awful moment, she wondered if this might have been flirtation from the salesman. She was entirely out of practice with flirtation since her husband had passed away. In all honesty, he hadn't been much for flirtation even during their decades of marriage. Regardless, flirtation of any sort would have been instant cause for dismissal of this oddly made gentleman. She was not running a bordello, nor did she ever hope to have a knocking on her chamber doors in the late hours as some gentleman sought out her company. She wouldn't have any of that sort of behaviour under her roof - she'd made it clear to all the ladies when they first moved in that gentleman callers could be seen in the receiving room, and only within the daylight hours with her there to serve as a chaperone. It had been almost a joke when she was saying it to them, as their only gentleman callers tended to be their sons, but the important thing was that she would not have the standards of her boarding house brought into question by any hint of potential iniquity.

Yet looking into the simple smile of the ape-like man in his pastoral black suit, there was no way that anything about him could be mistaken for frivolous or flirtatious. He was a step away from being a man of the cloth by her judgement, and it was a well-known fact that holy men such as that had no interest in the pleasures of the flesh.

She reached out to him with a smile of her own and marvelled as his grasping handshake completely enveloped not only her whole hand but her wrist, too, crushing the lace at her cuffs inadvertently. 'You are most welcome to stay with us for as long as you are in town.'

He looked ready to launch into a sermon as he pulled himself up to his full and monstrous height, as if brimstone and fire were about to burst forth from his lips. Instead, that same softness whispered out, 'Such kindness will not be forgotten when the time of judgement is upon us. It will be my pleasure to rest my weary head here while I do the Lord's work.'

Though she had nothing but trust for this oddly placid gentleman, she made a point not to be in his room at the same time as him. He looked the place over without comment on the cleanliness or the cramped conditions in which he would be kept. He was well-mannered to a fault. Even the widows often complained that they bumped against the close walls, and this man's shoulders were broader than the bedframe.

The only thing that took her by surprise was when he set aside his case and squatted down at the side of the bed, looking underneath it as though worried that he might find the bogeyman. He looked more like an ape than ever before, hunched down like that, but all it took was a glance and a cock of his head while he assessed the space before he sprang back up to his full height and gave her that same grin that she'd glimpsed before when he'd thought she wasn't looking. 'This will do nicely.'

Born Feral

Frances Nelson and James Ferral were a match made in Hell. Her daddy didn't want her running around with a Spanish immigrant, and James did everything he could to prove her daddy right. The only time the Nelsons got involved in the ongoing train wreck of their relationship was to stage a shotgun wedding in a quiet suburb of San Francisco when Frances turned up pregnant. A wedding that was barely attended by their respective families but overrun by the drunks and petty criminals that made up their social circle.

It was a wasted effort. James took his marital vows about as seriously as he took any other rules. He spent half the honeymoon slapping her around for turning his, less than romantic, propositions down and the other half whoring up and down the Barbary Coast.

Frances was no wide-eyed idealist hoping that her love could make a bad man good. She had not swallowed the Pentecostal gospel down on a Sunday morning for as long as she'd been able to stand up and say no to her mother. Forgiveness and redemption were foreign concepts to her. Her family had disowned her in a last-ditch attempt to teach her the error of her ways and bring her back under control, but instead it had served only to cut her entirely loose from any social obligations that she'd once felt. She washed down her morning sickness with liquor and entertained into the early hours of the morning in the flea-trap apartment that her husband had rented for them to start their family.

They saw each other most nights, even if the days were long and empty. James took on odd jobs, then drank or whored away the money he'd made before he came home to her. She had a pittance from him to pay rent and put food on the table, but she had neither the skills nor the inclination to be a housewife. When she did cook, it was barely edible, and on the few occasions that she produced something passable, James didn't come sauntering home until long after it had gone cold. By the end of her pregnancy, Frances had learned to pick her battles. If he was drunk, he wouldn't even remember what she was screeching at him as his fists fell. Waiting until morning meant that he'd have all morning to simmer on her complaints with a hangover jabbing at him before he could drink them away.

Earle Leonard Ferral was born on May 12, 1897. His mother had made it as far as the hospital before collapsing under the weight of the pain, but just a glance at her nether regions told the midwife everything that she needed to know about Frances's life. The baby had to force his way out through a crown of warts. Sores were open all around her vulva, leaking clear fluid onto the baby's head as he was trying to press out. The woman had syphilis, and judging by the roaring fever and the rash on her soles and palms, it was in an advanced stage.

There was every chance the sickness had infected the baby, too, or that it would pass to him through his mother's milk. For his own protection, he was taken from her, and she was left lying there in a hospital bed weeping and raging impotently that her precious son had been stolen away. When the father was finally identified and tracked down, he showed no hint of surprise to hear about his wife's condition. He had been infected with syphilis since before he'd even knocked her up, so making out that she'd been unfaithful seemed to be in bad taste. He held his son for the first time a day after the baby was born. It was the ugliest kid he'd ever seen, and he didn't know what to do with it. This was woman's work if ever he saw it.

The nurses fumbled through their excuses about why he had to push the rubber nipple into the brat's face and mix up this powder that smelled like puke, but he didn't really take it in. His wife had a perfectly fine set of tits for this job, why were they pestering him with it?

Back at home, he turned all of the childcare over to Frances as soon as possible. He didn't have the patience for it. Didn't have the temperament, either. He had money coming his way - he could tell from the way his palms were itching. He had to get back out there and live life as wild as he could while he still could.

Frances muddled through as best she could with the baby, trying to follow the doctor's instructions, but this wasn't something that came easy to her either, and the money for the powdered milk that they made her buy cut into her drinking money substantially. The baby cried all the time, and it made the walls quake around her, and she'd put her hands on its face and it would scream even more, and if she could just bring herself to choke the life out of the little bastard, then she could have a moment's peace, but she couldn't and she wouldn't, and as soon as those thoughts washed over her, they washed away again and she felt sick to her stomach. She knew that there was something wrong with her. Something that the doctors had tried to explain, but they'd given her medicine to help fight the bug she'd caught, so surely that meant she should be getting better, not worse. She was so hot all the time. She kept the windows open, but then she could hear bugs buzzing in and out, and the baby, she had to wrap up the baby to keep him warm, keep him away from the rain that was blowing through.

She didn't notice when James stopped coming home. There was already no money and too much to do, and the heat and the buzzing, and the baby needed milk, and the baby needed changing, and it was all too much. She had no time to worry about her husband when her baby needed her so much that she just wanted to smash its little screaming head against the walls.

James Ferral died in a gutter down by the docks. His infection took him, burning through his system and searing away whatever was left of his mind. Try as he might to drown it in liquor, there was no way to stem the tide.

When Frances died, it was quieter. She was still secluded away in her flea-trap apartment, still feeding her baby whenever some kind soul tossed a coin her way, still flinching away from every knock at the door since she was months behind on rent. Her face was being eaten away by bacteria. Her nose was almost gone. Her palms were covered in pustules, and she smeared the baby's swaddling with it every time she lifted him from his cot. He was six months old when his mother simply stopped coming when he cried. It was his shrieking that finally led the landlord to break down the door and find the corpse of Frances lying spread-eagled across the floor.

The baby lay there screaming as the police and doctors came and went. It lay there screaming as the body was carted off to the potter's field and her clothes and bedsheets were burned to prevent further infections spreading. Earle lay there screaming until finally, days after the last time he had been touched or held, a kindly face looked down at him and he was lifted into a motherly embrace by the grandmother he had never met. Jennie Nelson.

The Lord's House

Jennie was well on her way past middle-age when she adopted her grandson, but her youngest children, Willis and Lillian, were only ten and eight years his senior, so she hoped that he might still pass for hers and avoid any sort of awkward questions about his parentage. Her older children passed no comment on her decision; she was a woman of strong convictions and compassion, and since they no longer lived under her roof, they no longer felt they had a right to weigh in. Jennie's household was rigidly structured and entirely revolved around her devotion to the Pentecostal Church. It was puritan in the extreme, with no amount of indulgence or entertainment allowed. If the children must read, they would read the Word of God. If the children had energy enough to run around, then they could invest that energy more wisely cleaning the house or tending to the garden. This iron rule was the very thing that Frances had rebelled against so many years ago, leading her down the dark path that she had followed.

There were no shades of grey in Jennie's house, only the righteous and the sinful.

Neither Willis nor Lillian took to the wailing, dirty little beast that had been brought into their house of order, and they each took pains to avoid the onerous duty of caring for their orphan nephew. Jennie had no complaints about handling things herself. She enjoyed having a little baby to cradle in her arms again, even if it had cost her the life of one of her older children. To her mind, that child had already been lost to the Devil. The death of the body inevitably followed on from the death of the spirit, so there was nothing to mourn. She had a new soul to shelter, educate, and raise in the light of the Lord now, and she would make none of the mistakes with him that she had made with his mother. There would be no gaps between her fingers that this life might slip through. Her grasp on him would be airtight.

In public, he became known as Earle Nelson, his Spanish father's name stripped away from him along with any trace of his true ancestry. The only time that he ever heard about his mother or father was in the home, and even then it was only when he had committed some trespass and had to endure a lecture on the path of sin and the grim ends where it would lead him. Yet Willis and Lillian would still call the boy feral in their cruel private whispers. The boy knew nothing about living among civilised people. He could barely walk when he first came to their home, and even as he grew older, he'd lumber around on all fours like an ape instead of walking properly.

Worst of all were his table manners. While all the rest of the family said grace and waited patiently, it was all that the boy could do to contain himself. Then, when the time came to eat, he would dump olive oil all over his food to make it slick, and then shove his face into the plate to chomp the contents down in sodden chunks, gobbling it as fast as he could before the inevitable disciplinary caning began mid-meal. The sounds of his squeals and grunts became the accompaniment to every meal eaten in the house, yet still, he made no attempt to improve himself. Rather than reach for a fork and practice, he would rather suffer the beating and behave like a beast. Ferral by name, feral by nature.

Day by day, Jennie broke him, like you would a wild horse. Before he could read, he could recite Bible verse by rote, and when the time came for him to learn on his own, there was only one book that he was expected to study from. The initial jealousy of his aunt and uncle faded as they grew into their own lives outside of the home, and by the time that he was ten years old, they began to show some genuine affection for the little weirdo. All the things that had seemed so worthy of derision when they were younger now became endearing - a welcome break from the strict and stern upbringing of their mother. Where his bizarre behaviour, walking around the house on his hands and lifting the furniture with his teeth, had made him a laughingstock among his siblings and their friends before, now he provided some much needed freakshow levity to their otherwise drab lives.

When it came to his schooling, Earle's rather eccentric home education hampered him in no small way. He struggled with even the most basic school work and alienated both teachers and his fellow students with his fire and brimstone sermons, pronouncements of self-loathing, and ever more bizarre 'morbid' behaviour. He would set out to school dressed perfectly and return in tattered rags, as though he had traded his clothes with a hobo. This earned him many a beating, though he could never understand why. His attempts at play were always far too rough and rowdy for those around him, from biting and wrestling to snatching birds from their nests or playing chicken with oncoming trains, using his incredible agility to leap aside at the very last moment, mocking those few who were willing to indulge his habits for their cowardice in the face of death. He had no fear of death himself, for he would take his place in the Kingdom of the Lord when his time on Earth was done. He was a firm believer in the prophetic powers of the Bible, and in the concept of his own personal destiny, having been dictated from on high. He had a child's blind faith - the one thing in his mental makeup that his domineering grandmother had ever encouraged in him instead of trying to stamp out.

Willis's hand-me-down clothes kept the odd little boy dressed as he capered about the house, but it was only when the young man chose to donate his other belongings to the child that they exchanged hands. It wasn't that there was a concerted effort to deny Earle the same pleasures that they experienced, more that it simply did not occur to Jennie that such a thing would be necessary. Despite his nature, Earle put in all due efforts to be a good boy in the eyes of his carer. He did not ask for the things that he wanted, not ever. It had been drilled into him from the beginning that the roof over his head was an act of charity and that asking for more would be churlish. By the time that the boy was ten, it became clear to Willis that he was not getting free use of the things that children should have at their disposal, due to his mother's ongoing war on sin, so he handed down his old bicycle and then marvelled at the delight that Earle took in the gift.

With the uncanny balance that he used for his acrobatic tricks around the house, Earle had no trouble using the bike once the basic mechanics had been shown to him. It was the first possession that he considered to be truly his, and he delighted in showing it off to everyone that he met. He would race up and down the street at such a speed that it drew gasps from his audience, and before long, he started doing tricks with the bike that his uncle would never have even attempted. He was so delighted with his new toy that he forgot the all-important lessons of humility that Jennie had tried to instil in him. She did not beat the boy in the street, in full view of her neighbours, nor did she give him any rough treatment within her house. Instead, she waited and repeated her scripture to him at every opportunity, hoping that it would get through his thick skull. Pride comes before a fall.

When the fall came, it was more dramatic than any of them could have anticipated. Jennie had expected the boy to make a fool of himself, receive a reprimand from some figure of authority beyond her, and move on with his life sobered and sensible. What they had not anticipated was that Earle would be flying up and down the street when his wheel got caught in the street-car tracks, slowing him just enough for the street-car itself to round the corner and catch him a glancing blow to the head.

He fell to the cobblestones. His beloved bicycle was mangled beneath the street car, and every passenger disembarked to check if the child was alright. He most assuredly was not. A hole had been punched through his temple by the metal of the street car, and while he was still speaking and his eyes were still open, no part of his speech could be understood. It was as though he was suffering a Biblical affliction. He spasmed and twitched and spoke in tongues.

When he was dragged back into his grandmother's house by some of the children that he had been showing off for, she looked down on the boy with disdain as he wet himself. This was the inevitable end to his foolishness, and nobody should have been surprised by it. She shooed the children out of her house before turning her attentions to the boy, stripping him bare, cleaning him off, and then tucking him into bed. He would remain there for six days.

Psychotic Prodigy

When he finally stirred from his coma and staggered downstairs, he was crusted with sweat and excrement, dehydrated almost to the point of death. Before he was allowed a drink, he was sent out into the yard to be dashed clean with freezing water from the pump. He looked more like a beast now than ever before. The skin had closed over the injury to his temple in a pink pucker, but there was no telling how deep the damage had gone, or what poisons might be stuck inside. As he shivered and quivered beneath the buckets of water, he tried to remember what had happened to him and failed. He complained of a dreadful pain in his head, but Jennie put that down to the injury rather than anything that could be attended to. He was sat down at the table once he was cleaned off and given a stern talking down for his foolishness on the bicycle. He was told that it had been destroyed and that he would never be given one to ride again. Earle couldn't recall ever owning one, let alone any of the ill behaviour that he had supposedly committed while riding it.

The gaps in his memory proved ever more prevalent as time went by. The next day he rose, dressed himself, and set out for school, only to be turned away at the gates. He had been expelled from Aggasiz Primary School three years prior for his morbid and disruptive behaviour, with the head teacher dubbing him a psychotic prodigy. He could recall the majority of those three years easily enough, picking out other events, yet the fact that he had not been attending school had slipped his mind.

In the weeks and months after his injury, Earle's behaviour took a turn for the worse. He complained of constant headaches, fainted without cause or reason, and began to wet the bed, resulting in violent repercussions from his grandmother.

In attempts to self-medicate himself against the pains of both his head injury and her thrashings, he broke into her liquor cabinet and began working his way through the sherries and liqueurs that he found there - to little effect beyond making him queasy.

All of the things that he had been condemned for throughout his life, all of the things that he had wanted but shame or threats of damnation had frightened him away from, now came to the fore. He masturbated compulsively, day after day, night after night. Jennie would try to catch him in the act so that she could lambast and shame him properly, but he became entirely too clever for her liking. The blind trust that he had placed in his replacement mother figure was dead and gone, and she began to suspect that his collision with the streetcar had knocked the Lord's presence clean out of his head and that a demon had crawled inside the hole that was left while he lay indolent and slothful in his den of filth.

If self-abuse had been the limit of his sinful lusts, then it was likely that even one so firm-handed as his grandmother might have overlooked it with time, but Earle seemed intent on taking his perversion to new heights.

The first time that Jennie caught him lurking in the hallway after lights out, she thought nothing of it. The boy had always capered around the house at odd hours. Most often heading straight down to the kitchen where he would pilfer snacks for himself or fling himself headlong into another night-long marathon re-reading of the Book of Revelations. She forgave him at first for the second one - always too soft on him, as she had been his mother, and look where that got her. Yet this time he did not seem to be going anywhere at all. Instead, he was just lingering outside of Lillian's room, fidgeting but doing his damnedest to stay quiet. Jennie watched him for a time, unsure of what she was seeing, but when she began to tire and shifted her weight, the boy's bestial senses perked up and he abandoned all pretence at stealth, dropping to all fours and pounding off towards his room. Even that racket didn't disturb Lillian. She was still sitting there on her bed, halfway changed into her bedclothes with her top half exposed to the night air as she brushed out her hair.

Jennie pulled her daughter's door shut and stormed off to her room. The boy was peeping on his aunt as she changed. There could be no doubt about it. What was more, this could not be the first time that he had done it. He had known the exact time to come sneaking along and pressing his filthy little face up against the door frame. Incest. Voyeurism. Self-abuse. Perversion of the very worst kinds was taking place underneath her roof, and that sinful monstrous ape of a child was the one committing that perversion.

She should put him out. Cast him into the streets with no promise of forgiveness or repentance. She should defend her daughter's dignity from his lustful eyes and grasping hands. It would only be a matter of time before he started spraying the hallways with his sinful outbursts if she allowed this to go on. He had to be stopped dead in his tracks. Yet still, some sympathy stayed her hand. He was a young man, just coming into his man's growth, and that could lead to some mixed-up thoughts. If the boy had a father, then he could have given his son some discipline and order to his mind. Taught him the correct way to woo a lady, and that the sins that he was committing were not only a peril to his immortal soul but also a direct course to the venal corruption that had killed both of his parents in the bloom of their youth. If she cast him out now, she doomed another of her family to that same death, and as powerful as her convictions may have been, she still could not stomach that.

In the nights that followed, Jennie stalked the halls of their house, looking for any sign that the boy was out of bed, but she could find no evidence of further perversion. Even when she burst in on him in his room, all that she could rightly accuse him of was reciting Bible passages while lying in bed trying to settle into sleep.

It seemed that the head injury that he suffered had given young Earle an aversion to bright lights. He preferred to go outside only in the evening or early morning before the sun had reached its zenith, and even inside the home he seemed to shy away from the well-lit areas. His room began as a favoured retreat, but given his grandmother's near-constant intrusions there trying to make sure that he was not committing the sin of onanism once more, that soon fell out of his favour. Instead, he began retreating to the old house's expansive basement. The darkness soothed the pain in his head, and the cool seemed to lessen the fever that he felt burning at all times in his blood. He did not know whether some infection had taken root in his skull when he was injured and now bled out into every other part of him, or if these sinful lusts had always been within him, only contained by some lock that had now been shattered by the impact. It mattered little where his sinful desires came from - all that mattered was finding some way to sate them without heaping any more shame upon his already weary back.

The dark places of the world were where he felt he belonged. He could not be seen and judged down in the basement. He could live without the whole world being ready to crucify him for the slightest infraction. He lay down there in the dark, answering the voices that called out to him from the void and speaking the gospel until he was called upon to return to the light.

Pride and shame for her grandson wrestled with each other in the heart of Jennie Nelson. Since the accident, the boy had become ever stranger, whispering to himself and to people who were not there at all hours. Yet the one thing that remained consistent through all of his gibberings was his devotion to the Lord. Nine times out of ten, when she overheard his whispers more closely, they were recitations from the Bible.

It seemed to her that his prurient interest in the female body must have passed, thanks to the grace of God, and that now he had returned to the holy path. His ability to conceal his chronic masturbation more effectively with new tricks added to the faith that she had in him. Her nightly patrols eased and would have halted entirely if not for the curious fact that on her return to her chambers one night, she noticed a dull patch on the wood panelling by her door. Closer examination revealed that it had been scrubbed clean so thoroughly that the varnish had been removed from the wood. With the seed of suspicion planted in her mind, she tried to move on with her life, yet every night after getting changed for bed, she could not help but notice that her previously closed bedroom door was slightly ajar.

It was an abomination too shameful for her to even confront. She felt sick to her stomach to think of that filthy little ape manhandling himself and watching her in her state of undress. She began carrying a key to the interior doors on her person at all times, locking the bathroom when she went to bathe.

This guarded approach to her own body would eventually prove to be her undoing. After a slip in the tub, Jennie refused to call out for help, and when it did eventually come after she had slipped out of consciousness, it was entirely too late. The long hours of lying nude, drenched in cold water, resulted in a case of pneumonia that confined her to her bed through the coming month, until finally her strength failed her and she went to meet her maker.

Once again, Earle lost a parent.

Sins of the Father

Earle was fourteen years old when his grandmother passed away, and it was clear to everyone in the family that he was entirely unprepared for life on his own. His mother might have been happy to fly the nest at so young an age, but he lacked much of the basic understanding that would be required to live without supervision. The boy could barely dress himself, let alone seek employment. Yet none of his relatives wanted this odd little teenager in their lives. He did little to endear himself to them with his gibbering and fainting spells. Yet through all of this, there was one person who still cared for him. His aunt Lillian could still see the sweet boy who used to entertain her with his capering antics inside the broad, squat box of muscle that he had developed into.

All of her hopes about her judgement were fulfilled when the boy ambled into her house, still dressed in funeral blacks since nobody had told him to change. As he shuffled in, he looked as sober and beaten down as he ever had during Jennie's tyrannical rule, but a mere moment later, he seemed to fall into one of his faints, only to tumble over himself, then come up standing on his palms. Lillian let out a delighted laugh. The boy that she'd loved was still in there beneath the Bible verses and the misery.

 Her husband was not so taken with the boy, but the two of them never came into any sort of conflict, mostly because one of them was a grown man working a full-time job and the other was a capering man-child who disappeared into the streets every evening before the man of the house returned home for his supper.

It was never clear to Lillian where her nephew was going, but she made no attempts to stop him. In all the time that he lived with them, he never made any sort of dent in the allowance that was offered to him, despite having finally learned how to use money and her constant promises that there was nothing sinful about spending money on the things that he wanted. He came home happy and unscathed from his outings, even when they lasted several days at a time, so what could she possibly complain about?

Earle liked to roam the city and beyond, doing what others might have called communing with nature. Away from built-up areas and judging eyes, he was free to do as he liked, move as he liked. In solitude, he found some comfort, or at least enough peace to hear all of the voices that spoke only to him. The ones that Jennie had said were demons trying to tempt him. They said that the Devil could quote scripture when it served his purposes, but Earle could not understand what the purpose of the endless recitation of Revelations in his mind might be serving beyond driving him to despair. He would sleep rough when he was outside of the city, finding hunting hides to shelter in or sometimes letting himself into the cabins that sat empty and unlocked throughout most of the year. His faith in the divine order was in no way diminished. If he tried one of those cabin doors and found them to be locked, then it was a sign that God wanted him to sleep out under the stars that night. He had no tussles with the local wildlife - even predators could sense the danger contained in his compact body, even if he himself did not yet realise it.

Within the city, he roamed without challenge from any quarter. The police overlooked him for his well-tailored clothes, and the criminals overlooked him for his Biblical gibbering. Nobody wanted a reputation for beating on a holy man or a madman. He walked through his life in San Francisco completely invisible to those around him. Lost in his own daydream world with an accompanying chorus of heavenly voices. Even with his wallet full of cash, nobody bothered Earle.

His self-abuse remained a constant throughout this time, but nobody was around to complain that he spent his private time furiously masturbating, not anymore. Whether in the wild places, the back alleys, or the privacy of his room, the glimpses of nudity that he had witnessed through his childhood seemed to haunt him. Lillian wouldn't have known how to address the situation even if she were aware of it.

Worked into a frenzy of sexual frustration, Earle eventually found his way to the same streets where he had been born, the same old haunts that had consumed the lives of both his parents. He drank to quiet the pain in his head and the voices that haunted him in the same hole-in-the-wall speakeasy joints that his parents had frequented. He slept in the same alleyways that his father had lain in when the liquor overtook him. He crossed their paths over and over again, never knowing that he was treading in their footprints. All of which led him inevitably to the Barbary Coast.

From Portsmouth Square to the docks at Buena Vista Cove, Earle became a familiar sight. He never gambled, he never visited a dance hall, and he never stepped inside any saloon with a tune playing. He still believed all of his grandmother's stories about the sinful nature of secular music and the rattle of the Devil's bones when you rolled the dice. He could not be tempted by these worldly pleasures. For many, the ambling and rambling man, clothed always in black, became something of a local landmark. The only kind of preacher who would sully himself by visiting Pacific Street was a madman, and that had a certain poetic justice to it.

He became a favourite of the prostitutes out parading their wares because his very presence seemed to dissuade their more violent customers from acting out. His protruding brows were drawn down. His broad shoulders strained against the fabric of his suit. This odd little teenager plodding up and down protected them more efficiently than every pimp and paid-up policeman in the whole city.

Of course, the affection translated directly into many offers of business. Nobody expected him to say yes - in fact, making him blush and bumble on citing scripture was much more entertaining for the prostitutes than yet another awkwardly fumbling teenager in some dank alleyway. So, when the day came that Earle screwed on his courage and said yes to one of the old madams on a street corner, it was met with surprise. Even when she told him her price, considerably more than she expected to make in a day, he was not dissuaded.

In the sweat-stained back room of a brothel, Earle Nelson had sex for the first time in his life. His huge hands clamped down on the withered shoulders of the ageing whore, grinding her bones with every thrust of his hips. Making her weep and struggle against him when, even after he had reached his completion, he just wouldn't stop, hammering on and on. Eyes rolled up into his head. Hallelujah on his lips from start to finish.

She did not put about the word to the others in the oldest profession about Earle's rough treatment. She didn't expect that the wannabe holy man would have the shamelessness to come back, roaming those streets again. She was wrong. Shame was Earle's bread and butter, swallowed down with every waking moment. He was so saturated with shame that he could not differentiate between the guilt that he should feel for glancing at a pretty girl in the street and the guilt that he should feel for squeezing his hands around the throat of an elderly whore in the alleyway between a dance hall and a gin joint. He knew that he was a sinner. He had been born a sinner, child of a whoremonger and an imbecile - that had always been what he was told.

The self-loathing that simmered within him now was no different from what he had felt every moment of his life for as long as he could remember. The only difference was that now the burning of his lusts had been quieted.

Earle began to dip more heavily into his allowance, still only touching a fraction of what he was offered. He did not have the refined tastes that would have required expense. His drinks were the cheapest rotgut whiskey. His whores were the ugly, the elderly, and the sickly - the women that all the other customers of the Barbary Coast overlooked until their purses grew too light to avoid them.

His roaming outside of the city came to a complete halt, and his long periods of absence from Lillian's home could now be accounted for entirely in the doss-houses and the docklands. All was well in Earle's little world, or at least all that could be well in a doomed world full of damned souls. All of his needs were being met, all of his worries were being dampened with liquor. He probably could have gone on like that forever were it not for the risks involved in such a lifestyle finally catching up to him.

Firmly believing that his body was already mortified with sin, Earle took little notice of it, cleaning himself as his grandmother had directed, but otherwise paying no heed to its appearance or the changes enacted upon it by time. He had ignored the growth of hair on his legs, chest, back, and arms, even when it crept down to protrude from his cuffs. He had ignored the spread of his shoulders, the swelling of his muscles, and the halt of his upward growth. As his body transformed into that of a man, he paid it no heed. When it itched, he would scratch it. When it hurt, he would take care to avoid damaging it further. But that was the extent of his self-care.

So, it fell to one of the prostitutes that he frequented in a brothel to stop him from pounding away at her as usual when she saw him in a state of undress and noted the pus drooling out of open sores on his genitals. She would not have him - none of the whores in the house would have him. None of the whores in the Barbary Coast were willing to lie down with a man so clearly afflicted with venereal disease, and thanks to the shame that had been imparted to him by his grandmother, he didn't dare to seek out medical care to deal with his situation.

Crimes and Institutions

Suddenly, the appeal of the city entirely faded for Earle. He packed up his few belongings and took to the road, disappearing from his aunt's house for weeks at a time instead of mere days. This did not come without some relief for Lillian and her husband. As much as she cared for the boy, there was no denying that life was easier when he was not around, and given his curious physicality, nobody felt that he was in any real danger out in the world despite his rather stunted mental capabilities.

Hopping trains was the easiest way to get around in those days, so Earle made good use of the rails to put distance between himself and the painful memories of home. He lacked the courage to go roaming too far from everything that he had ever known, but within the state of California, he felt entirely at home. For many months following his exile from the Barbary Coast, Earle roamed the wild places of his world in solitude.

All of that freedom was soon to be stripped away from him, however. His old habit of letting himself into abandoned cabins to sleep through the night came back to bite him when he wandered into an occupied one in Plumas County, Sierra Nevada. The family that had arrived for a weekend outside of the relative bustle of East Quincy were startled when the filthy, lumbering hobo opened the door to the cabin and walked in as though he owned the place, and Earle was held at gunpoint until the local police could be summoned to take him into custody. So far from home, he had nobody to speak up for him, and with his limited mental capabilities, he was incapable of standing up for himself.

The judge took his muttering and mumbling throughout his trial to be signs of disrespect, so for the awful crime of walking through an unlocked door, the young man was sentenced to two years in San Quentin State Penitentiary in the summer of 1915, at the age of eighteen. His time in prison was untroubled. Once more, he found himself in regular receipt of meals and shelter with no need for effort on his part, and as an added bonus, the medical examination that he received on arrival to the penal system revealed the issues that he was having with his penile systems. A treatment was prescribed and consumed, and before long, the lumbering, ape-like man was known throughout the prison as a compulsive masturbator.

Soft-spoken despite his muscular build, Earle was overlooked in most of the internal strife within the prison. His devotion to faith, quoting of scripture, and silent approach was enough to earn him the respect of many of San Quentin's violent offenders. As for the rest, the fact that the man was clearly dangerous and unhinged managed to keep them at arm's length. Earle managed to serve out a year of his sentence without so much as a ruffled feather, and in a time of horrific overcrowding, that was all that was required to earn him a spot in front of the parole board.

Like the prison population, the parole board were taken in by all of Earle's Biblical recitations and clear signs of mental illness. He was not considered to be a threat to others, and given the nature of his crime had been almost entirely accidental on his part, they were quite happy to discharge him from the prison on September 6, 1916.

For the first time, the shame that had always followed Earle had good reason to influence those around him. His aunt had tolerated him in her home when he was merely a bizarre soft head, but now that he was a criminal to boot, there was no talk of him returning to her care. That suited Earle just fine. He sat down with his aunt as though he were a visiting relative, gathered up a suitcase of the few items of clothing he had not destroyed, and departed in due course, both from her home and from the city of San Francisco itself. The world was his oyster - thanks to the help he'd received from his new friends in the criminal underworld.

Prison had taken an innocent but impressionable young man and locked him in close quarters with professional crooks. With his longing for freedom, it was hardly a surprise that the free-wheeling life that those criminals advocated should appeal to him. As he made his way across California, his pockets were never empty. The little nest egg that Lillian had slipped to him so that he did not struggle remained barely touched as he continued to do what he had always done - letting himself into secluded rural properties at night. The only difference now was that he would strip them of valuables rather than camp out in them, catching up on sleep while he was hopping trains rather than committing to a night's rest and sleeping rough too close to the scenes of his crimes.

This new routine suited him well. He was still uncomfortable when exposed to daylight, preferring to be out and about under the cover of darkness, not only for the benefits that it provided him in his burgeoning burglary career but also because it eased the pain in his head. Sadly, his nocturnal habits also meant that when he tried the same tricks that worked fine on the abandoned country homes of wealthy townsfolk within built-up areas, he would come into contact with the homeowners, startled awake.

It did not take long before his newly learned criminal behaviour got him into trouble. In Stockton, San Joaquin County, he was caught breaking into a townhouse by the police before the owners had even been disturbed from their slumber. He was carted off to stand trial almost immediately, receiving a sentence of six months for petty larceny on the basis of the stolen goods that he already had on his person. It was served out in the local jail rather than one of the larger penitentiaries in the state, then he was cut loose all over again towards the midpoint of 1917.

With his medical issues resolved, Earle became intent on pursuing his old favourite hobby of whoring once more but, unwilling to go near to his old haunts, he headed down to Los Angeles to seek out new prospects. There was a burgeoning scene of prostitution in 1917 LA, but after bail, court costs, and general bad luck, Earle had barely two pennies to rub together to partake of the cavalcade of flesh. He needed to refill his wallet fast, and he had only one trade that he could rely on to bring money his way.

Earle was arrested the day after he arrived in LA for burglary, and with his prior convictions, the sentence this time was far less generous. He wasn't liable to see sunshine again until the '20s had roared by. The voices that he heard in his head began to tell him to kill himself rather than endure imprisonment. He spoke openly to his jailors in the Los Angeles County Jail about his suicidal intentions, saying that if he were not set free, then he would find some sharp object and open up his veins rather than endure any further curtailing of his God-given right to roam free. The guards took this as more of a joke than a threat. If he were to die on their watch, it just meant that their workload lightened.

With no hope of salvation from on high, Earle instead turned to lower places. There were already several concerted efforts to break out of the prison underway, and Earle's immense strength and limited height proved to be an advantage to those attempting to tunnel out under the prison walls.

The darkness and the dank air reminded Earle of the basement back home in Jennie Nelson's house, and his recitations from the Bible lifted the spirits of those who dug alongside him. They need not have bothered. In the time that it would have taken them to reach the wall above, Earle had already dug his way through to the surface.

He parted ways with his new companions in crime just outside the prison walls, scattering to the winds to avoid detection and disrupt pursuit. Their absence wasn't even noted in the bustling prison for almost a week, by which time they were all long gone. Only a few months of his sentence had been served, yet here he was, walking free and easy in a suit that he had stolen off a washing line.

It may have seemed to Earle that time stood still when he was in his confinement, but the truth was that history was marching on at a rapid pace during his dalliances with the law. In April of 1917, America entered the First World War officially, declaring war on Germany and enacting a selective draft to fill out the many uniforms that its burgeoning economy had already paid for. By the time that Earle found his freedom, the world that he was escaping into had changed. Something resembling discipline was spreading out through the nation as it pulled together in pursuit of victory. The raucous partying that young Earle had looked upon with judgement and no small amount of envy throughout the years had taken on an entirely different tone, with all the brave boys having one last hurrah before setting out to enlist.

This was a calling. The kind that Earle had always longed for in his heart of hearts. A righteous cause, a devilish foe, camaraderie and adventure. As soon as he was certain that the prison was not hunting after him, he went to the nearest military base and signed himself up.

The three weeks that followed were bizarre for everyone involved. "Earle Ferral" blasted through the physical aspects of his military training effortlessly, but his ability to maintain that discipline outside of exercise was severely lacking. He would not march in time with the rest of his unit. He would not rise from his cot when it was the allotted time. He would spend unholy amounts of time in the showers after lights out. The other men in his billet could not sleep for the sound of his constant muttering and murmuring. He was the most hated man in his whole unit, yet in the spirit of camaraderie in those heady days, there was none of the usual bullying or jockeying for position that you might expect. Instead, those higher up in the chain of command took note of the morale damage that this muscular young recruit was dealing to his own unit and decided to push him out the side door.

Every miserable duty on the base became Earle's. Digging and cleaning latrines seemed to have no impact on him as he cared nothing for hygiene, and hard labour washed off his back like water to a duck. The only thing that seemed to trouble him were long stints of doing nothing. The nervous energy bound up inside of him always sought an outlet, so guard duty ended up as the best way to torment him. Seeking to preserve something resembling a normal sleep schedule for the other recruits, Earle was placed on night-time guard duty at one of the base's gates. Completely alone and unobserved with nothing to do for upwards of eight hours every night. Nothing to keep him company but the moon above and his boredom.

Houdini

It took three days of solitude and silence before he deserted, strolling off into the night. Military police could easily have gone and chased him down, but this was the outcome that his superior officers had been hoping for all along, a way to be rid of Earle without having to go through the tedium of due process. For a time, Earle vanished.

The next time that he resurfaced after his long walk through the night was in Salt Lake City, Utah. This was a place unlike anywhere Earle had ever been or seen before. A city built on values completely different to his own, yet mirroring them in so many ways. There was a criminal element in Salt Lake City, the same as in any city, but the religious hypocrisy that he had always borne witness to seemed to be absent. The upstanding gentleman of this society could not be found whoring again by Sunday afternoon. Here, he saw that people could actually live up to the values that his grandmother had struggled so hard to instil in him, and it filled him with self-loathing.

Almost as soon as he arrived, he wanted to get out of town again. Taking the shortest route to the coast, he signed up to the US Navy at the stand they had on Main Street, and he was on a train headed for the coast with all the other recruits before the sun had even dipped towards the horizon.

San Francisco. He'd been running from that place for so long that it had gone ahead and changed in his absence. The Barbary Coast had been shrunk down to just a few blocks. The Navy, which had always maintained a presence in the city, now dominated the shorefront, with all the old doss-houses where Earle used to sleep off his moonshine now converted into billet space as the war machine ground to life. The names of the streets that Earle walked were familiar, but none of the faces looked the same. He need not have worried about being recognised by old friends or relatives - the man who'd come home and the boy who'd left barely resembled each other. The face might have been the same, but the slicked-back hair and the hulking body were foreign. The animalistic potential of Earle's frame had been fulfilled, and now he looked every bit the gorilla that his aunt and uncle had once mockingly called him, his dark Navy uniform doing nothing to hide his prodigious bulk.

Assigned to the galley, since he lacked aptitudes that would be helpful in the running of the ship elsewhere, Earle soon found that the chores involved were too dull. He would wander off from his station only to receive a stern talking down, and he would linger in his bunk until long after he was meant to be in attendance at his station. It did not take long before he abandoned his post and sank back into the morass of the San Francisco underworld. Navy officers did attempt to pursue him this time, but it was to no avail. The man knew the city like the back of his hand.

For two months, he lurked around the Bay Area as the war that all had hoped could be won decisively grew in scale to consume the whole world. With all the old opportunities for easy money rapidly drying up, Earle re-enlisted under yet another pseudonym, this time as a medical corpsman. When he decided to abandon that post after several months, he was successfully intercepted by military police before he'd made it a mile, and they proceeded to interview him about his reasons for abandoning his country in her time of need before they brought him back to face punishment. He claimed that 'burning about his anus bothered him', leading the arresting officers to leap to the logical conclusion that Earle had been on the receiving end of some of the buggery that was currently plaguing many branches of the US Military. He was suffering from the rather unpleasant side effects of yet another venereal disease that he'd picked up on the greatly reduced Barbary Coast during his downtime. Rather than bringing him back onto the base and risking the embarrassment associated with stories of this behaviour coming out, they cut him loose.

In 1918, Earle joined up with the Navy once more, but by now his deteriorating mental state was abundantly clear to everyone around him. He lay in his bunk all through the day and the night, compulsively reciting the Book of Revelations from memory and claiming that the Great War was a sign of the end times. This was, unsurprisingly, another impediment to ship's morale, so rather than flogging the man and trying to get him back on the straight and narrow, the Navy resorted to the one thing that every other institution and family that Earle had ever experienced had failed to do. They sent him to a doctor to examine his mental health.

Napa State Mental Hospital was both Earle's salvation and his prison. It was here that he was able to speak truthfully for the first time about his life and his experiences - the only time that he was able to be honest with others and himself about the combination of swirling dark influences that had led him to his current state of self-loathing and doomsaying.

Blood tests revealed previous infections with multiple sexually transmitted diseases, and further tests and interviews revealed that his heavy alcohol usage, which had started at the age of thirteen, had finally come to a halt seven months prior to being confined. This was not a moral choice on the part of Earle. Rather, he said that the drink no longer gave him any respite from the pains that he suffered.

The scarring on his left temple could still be seen beneath the grime, and the headaches continued to haunt him. Even during his brief intake interview, he nearly fainted twice as the pain overtook him. It was impossible to tell whether his pain was genuine or some manufactured attempt to manipulate the doctors, but the head injury was considered to be the root cause of his problems rather than the stifling religious upbringing, which seemed to have had a considerably more impactful effect on his psyche.

Within the hospital, Earle was liked well enough by staff but never trusted. He would get up and leave his room at all hours, easily tracked down by the sound of his apocalyptic rambling echoing behind him wherever he went.

He was relentless in his wandering, and eventually, he managed to slip out of the building unnoticed in the dead of night. Recaptured on the grounds, he saw his freedom curtailed even further, and the Medieval 'treatments' that he had only undergone haphazardly before stepped up to a full-time regimen of torment that he silently endured. It was hardly a surprise to the staff that he made another escape attempt after only a few days of that unpleasantness.

There was no mad rush to recapture the escaped mental patient, given that his records showed that he was not 'violent, homicidal or destructive'. Yet even with a rather anaemic approach to hunting Earle down, he was soon recovered from the streets of San Francisco and returned to his cell. Nicknaming him Houdini, the staff began to take bets on when he would make his next attempt at breaking out. Those who bet sooner rather than later were rewarded.

On his third breakout, it was apparent to the Napa staff that trying to drag Earle back over and over again was a waste of their time and energy when there were people with real problems that they had a chance of helping. Earle was fundamentally harmless in their opinion. He had absorbed all the lessons of the Good Book at a young age, and that was sure to curb any dark desires that passed through his head. He was discharged from both the Navy and the hospital in absentia, with a mark on his file describing him as 'much improved'. Just like the section that described him as 'non-violent', this particular descriptor was soon to be proven entirely false.

At a loose end in the city where he had been born and raised, Earle began to re-tread old footsteps once again, roaming through all his old stomping grounds and trying to recognise the bones of the city underneath the patina of time. It was not long before he found himself lingering outside of the old Nelson house, looking up at the only place that he had ever truly felt at home, with a sober expression on his face. Perhaps it was that sullen look, as well as the particular location, that made a woman in the street stop and look at him more closely before drawing the vacant brute of a man into her embrace. Earle leaned into her arms without a clue as to what was happening. His world had not included any sort of softness or kindness for so long that it now felt alien to him. It was only when she drew back and he was able to look down into the face of his Aunt Lillian that he knew her.

With nowhere to go and no plans for his future, Earle followed her home like a little lost puppy. While he had never looked back since parting ways with his family, Lillian had been riddled with guilt and regrets from the moment that he left town. She felt like she had let the legacy of her mother's philanthropy down, and she felt like she had abandoned Earle when he needed support the most. All of these things were technically true, of course, but did not take into account the myriad ways in which young Earle had transformed through the years.

His old room was now a child's nursery. The grim and silent home that he had once haunted was now filled with life. Earle moved through it all like the spectre of the dark and forgotten past, shying away from the attention of his uncle and cousins and lingering in the halls instead of stepping through doorways into the light. When it became apparent that he had nowhere else to go, Lillian tried to settle him in a guest bedroom but come morning he had vanished. There was a hunt through the house that Lillian's husband hoped would be fruitless but eventually uncovered Earle curled up in a corner of the basement beside the furnace. If it had been winter and the fire lit, he would have scalded himself badly, and he would have been impossible to hear muttering his ceaseless prayers over the sound of the burning coals. A cot was set up for him in the basement in the days that followed, and that would remain his home for the coming months. He would slink in unnoticed and slip out unnoticed by all the people in the house above, his only interaction with them being his aunt Lillian coming down to speak to him for a few minutes before she went off to her bed, stroking the oiled hair back from his face and telling him that he was loved.

Bride of the Beast

Her husband was less inclined to serve as a nursing home for the criminal and the deranged. He wanted Earle out of his house and away from his children, but he was not without empathy. His strongly worded suggestions to his wife were not about kicking the man into the street, but rather about helping him to find his feet and start a new life for himself. Lillian bought this line and immediately set about finding her nephew a job where his limited capabilities would not be an impediment but a boon.

Earle was reluctant to take on work within the city for fear of crossing paths with one of the military branches that he had abandoned in his nation's hour of need, but a janitorial position out at St Mary's hospital on the outskirts suited him perfectly. He was registered with the hospital as Evan Louis Fuller and set to work immediately. Not only did the job provide him with a steady income, but it also provided him a source of endless prurient interest and a home much like the one that he'd most recently enjoyed - a fold-out cot in the dark of the basement, kept warm through his day's sleep by the clanking of the steam pipes.

While his mental state had not improved since the last time that he was committed, his re-affirmed relationship with his aunt had brought Earle some degree of mental stability. She was an anchor to stop his flights of fancy from carrying him off, and while he could still be heard reciting Bible verses everywhere that he went throughout the hospital, it actually served as some comfort to the patients and staff. Evan became known as a beacon of calm in a place that was often fraught, and if he were a little simple in the head, then all should aspire to be so simple.

It was during his rounds in the early evening as he brushed and mopped the hallways that he first heard the crackling laughter of Mary Martin. Mary was a fifty-eight-year-old spinster who had spent her entire adult life working in the hospital without any hope of advancement or relief. She remained in the same administrative role that she had taken on before the turn of the century and would continue to plod on in that same role for the rest of her life unless interrupted. She took pleasure in the small things - the good company of the other girls in the administrative block, the handsome young janitor who would linger in the doorway for as long as he dared, staring in at her with open admiration in his eyes.

At first, Mary could not believe that his interest in her was anything romantic. After all, she was old enough to be his mother. Yet as the days and weeks rolled on with his big doleful eyes fixed on her each time he passed, she couldn't help but feel a little flattered. It had been said around the hospital that the man was a little simple, but if you had gone fifty years waiting for a more complex man to show some interest, then perhaps that wouldn't be too much of an impediment.

When she finally caught up to this young Evan and asked him to join her for a coffee in the cafeteria, he seemed anything but simple. There were untold depths behind his dark eyes. In the long moments of silence between them, when he could not meet her gaze, he had the look of a troubled man, yet he could recite scripture for any occasion and seemed to be well-liked by everyone. He bore the marks of a rough life on his skin, and of hard labour beneath his boiler suit. Evan was a man with a history, a man who likely could have had his pick of younger women if he took the time to talk to them, yet here he was talking to her all evening long.

Even after their first coffee together, Mary still wasn't clear on whether Evan's intentions were romantic or not, but at least his lurking had stopped. He would come to see her when her shifts were ending, or when she had a break, and the sight of the two of them sitting together became commonplace enough that nobody felt any need to comment. Nobody outside of the pair really knew what was going on within the relationship, but so long as they minded their own business, that didn't much matter to either one of the infatuated duo.

Mary began to revive her long-dormant instinct for romance when Evan began pressing a dry-mouthed kiss to her cheek before they parted ways, but it wasn't until she finally took the initiative and turned her lips to meet his that she knew for certain what Earle really wanted. That darkness she saw boiling behind his eyes even when he was at peace - she knew now that it was passion.

Of course, Mary was a devout Catholic, so she was careful to keep his passion held at arm's length. She had to do little more than tut or look at Evan with disdain to stop his grasping hands in their tracks. She made it clear early in their relationship that she had no intention of having sex before marriage, and Evan apologised for making her uncomfortable. He was truly a gentleman from a bygone age. The kind that Mary had never hoped to meet in these sinful and turbulent times.

Only a few months into their relationship, Evan began speaking to Mary more seriously of marriage. Not out of passion, but out of a genuine desire to spend every waking moment in her company. Mary spent some time trying to put him off, to list off all the reasons that the two of them should not be together. They would never have children. She would die long before him. He had a young man's vigour, while hers faded more with each day. She rattled through every excuse not to be together, but Evan wiped all of them away with his simple declaration of love. He did not care what others thought. He did not care about the future. All that existed for him was the moment that they were living in now, and in that moment, he loved her.

She threw one final impediment in his path before finally taking the ring that he kept trying to push onto her finger when they were holding hands. They would only be wed if it could be in a Catholic ceremony. She knew that Evan had not been raised Catholic from the way that he recited his scriptures and interpreted them during their healthy debates over the state of affairs across the world. It should have been an impassable barrier, yet Evan hopped the hurdle without pause. He was open to any and all religious experiences. He had no preference for a sect or church in particular - all that he cared about was that God could look down and witness their bonding.

It was hard to argue with that kind of blind devotion, so the two of them were married in August 1919. Just as Mary's family had thought that she would never find someone and settle down, so too did Evan doubt his ability to find somebody to love and care for him.

With the ceremony over, Evan took his new bride back to the apartment that she had rented since she was eighteen years old and carried her over the threshold. It was the final moment when she still believed that her fairy-tale marriage was coming true.

Their very first night together was arduous. Evan treated her like she was his whore, doing whatever he pleased with her body while she lay there too mortified to object. In the light of day, Evan seemed to be himself once more, kind and clever. Soft as cotton wool when he placed a delicate kiss on her cheek as though he had not spent hours desecrating her flesh throughout the night. Mary did not know enough to object. She suspected that what she had endured was unusual, but she had no frame of reference, and she was by far too ashamed to ever speak to anyone about it. For all that she knew, this was simply the duty of a wife to endure and never speak about. That very night, Evan came for her again, but she was prepared. She spun him a story about being too tired, about being worn out from the night before, about the pain that he had left her in. None of these things seemed to put Evan off, yet when she sternly told him to stop, he obeyed. In this as in the rest of their marriage, when he acted the naughty child and she the domineering mother, he slipped into the role comfortably.

When she would not have sex with him, Evan took matters into his own hands. Once again, Mary was absolutely mortified as he lay there in the bed beside her masturbating and grunting like an ox. This time, however, she had scripture to guide her. She knew that what he was doing to himself was a sin, and she felt that he had no grounding to argue otherwise. She expected theological debate when she confronted him over breakfast but was treated instead to a harsh dose of her new reality that stung more than the foul spray that she had felt up the back of her nightgown in the darkness. Evan simply said, 'You wouldn't do what a wife is meant to.'

It was hard to hold on to any anger with Evan in the daylight hours, when he was so openly adoring that even strangers paused to comment on how deeply in love the odd couple had to be. That same affection bubbled over all too quickly into jealousy when he saw other men speaking to his wife. At first it was funny, even adorable, to see him scowling every time any other man spoke to Mary, whether it was postman, milkman, or colleague at work. It was clear to everyone that the simple fellow saw his wife as the most desirable woman in the world despite her age, and that his little spats of frowning simply reflected that. What they did not see was the property damage that resulted from those rages.

He did not hit Mary. He would never hit Mary. It was unconscionable to hurt his mother. Wife. Not mother. Wife. He had to remind himself of that. Instead, he turned his rage on their rather meagre belongings. More than once he had to plaster up holes that he had punched in the wall after seeing Mary talking with a stranger. More than once, they'd had to discreetly replace an item of furniture that he'd broken down to matchsticks and fluff with his bare hands.

Most disgusting of all to Mary were the accusations of infidelity that sprung so readily to her husband's lips once they were behind closed doors. Gratuitous descriptions of the things that he imagined her doing with other men. Things so grotesque that even he hadn't attempted to force them on her in their bedchamber. Every one of these accusations came back to haunt her after nightfall, when rejecting Evan would unleash the same torrent of abuse all over again - of course she didn't want him after she had been fucking every man in town behind his back all day. If it was a pressure tactic, it could have been judged a success. She suffered through more of his 'lovemaking' to avoid these rants than she ever had before. Sadly, it was not an abusive act by a reasoning mind but rather an expression of the sickness that was deeply rooted in Earle. One day he returned home from his shift to see a man seated at his spot by the kitchen table, and it was as though all of his worst nightmares had sprung to life. He walked right past the man without a word, heading for the cutlery drawer and the lethally sharp knives that Mary used to dice and slice their dinners. Mary arrived back in the room right in the nick of time to introduce Evan to his brother-in-law before blood could be spilt.

Evan was polite and discreet through the whole evening, chatting away with his usual reserved nature, never quite giving way to small talk. He seemed to be quite respectable to Mary's brother, always carefully considering every answer in a way that most of his generation wouldn't. While he had been quite ready to dislike Evan, instead he found a grudging respect for the man who had won his sister's heart. They parted ways with a firm handshake. Even Mary firmly believed that all was well, and the door swung shut. Then the recriminations began. She could not understand why his voice was raised. She could not understand what he could possibly be angry about.

It was only when his old rhetoric about other men came to the fore that she realised what he was implying about her relationship with her brother. She was appalled and disgusted, but that expression of emotion convinced Earle that he had caught her in a deception. He doubled down on his character assassination, not only accusing her of incest – and suggesting that her long years of spinsterhood were punctuated by her physical needs being met by her own brother – but going into excruciating detail about what he believed that his elderly wife, and her elderly brother, had been doing before Evan arrived home.

This went on and on. Every time that Mary left the house, she could expect to come home to a passionate tirade about her infidelity. Yet even this was not the strangest part of her marriage. Evan would not wash himself properly, and when he did engage in any sort of hygiene, it was in truly bizarre manners, such as pouring glasses of water over his toes at the kitchen table.

One thing that she never had to demand from him was that he change his clothes. He would do that by himself for no discernible cause, changing from perfectly respectable clothing into ridiculous costumes like a plaid golfer's outfit, a sailor's uniform, or even his own shoddily home-made suits that he assembled by butchering Mary's dresses.

Yet still, Mary was a good Catholic woman with no intention of divorcing her husband. It did not matter if he was strange, or rude, or broke things. It did not matter if he dressed like a buffoon and made her a laughingstock among her friends. Their marriage had been sanctified by God, and no man or woman was going to part them.

In no small part, Mary tried to justify Evan's bizarre behaviour in the context of his health problems. Headaches still plagued him, and he would often have dizzy spells. This integral weakness within the burgeoning mass of muscles reminded Mary that for all that Evan was a surprisingly wise young man, he was only human and fallible. That his actions and the awful things he said to her were expressions of that fallibility. She did what she could to keep him happy.

In the Shadow of the Valley of Death

The insufferable weakness that had plagued Earle throughout his life flared back into action almost five months into his marriage. The headaches grew worse. The dizzy spells and fainting became more and more consistent. Even as Mary worked around the clock to bring him comfort in all the myriad ways that only a mother and a lover combined could, they still grew more and more intense. Eventually, he had a bout of dizziness while repainting a section of the hospital's roof, and he tumbled down from his ladder, striking his head on the ground and slipping into a coma for three days. During this time, his adoring wife sat by his bedside, doing all that she could to bring him comfort, but it was to no avail until eventually one morning, without warning, he woke up and walked right out of the hospital, head still bound up in bandages.

He came home to Mary, but the man who walked through her door was not the man that she had fallen in love with. All of his religious mania had now come to the forefront. He talked at great length about the Great Beast of Revelations that was coming to herald the end of the world. He ranted and raved, quoting scripture ceaselessly to prove to Mary that the end times were upon them. Mary, who had been raised in the rather less apocalyptically inclined Catholic sect, was confused and horrified by this bizarre turn.

Even once he had stripped away his bandages and dressed in his best black suit as though he were going to church, nothing about Evan returned to normal. Worse yet, he seemed to have forgotten his name. He called himself Earle and spoke about being in the Navy and the Army, about lying awake at night in a prison cell listening to the angels telling him to slit his wrists open and bathe the world in his blood.

The horrifying thing about each and every one of these bizarre rambling tales was that Mary realised that any one of them could have been true. She had no idea who the man that she'd married really was. The secrecy that had seemed so mysterious and appealing when they first began courting was now a source of mounting horror. He could be anyone. He could be the man who heard angels. He could be the janitor at the hospital. He could be a hardened criminal. She had no way of deciphering which part of his ramblings were the truth and which were the product of his fevered imaginings.

That night she was thankful when he did not come to bed or try to lay with her because her faith had been shaken so profoundly that she did not think she could fake her way through another of his amorous encounters.

When she rose in the morning, he was still seated at their kitchen table, looking out at the sun rising and muttering away to himself. There was no expectation that either one of them would turn up to work. Indeed, the hospital had only just realised that Evan was no longer in the ward. They had the day to themselves. Usually, Evan would have used this time to proposition her before they went out about town, but it hardly seemed appropriate on this day. He barely seemed to notice that his own wife was in the room with him.

As the day dragged on and Mary went through the motions, she wondered when the other shoe was going to drop, when Evan or Earle or whoever was lurking in her kitchen was going to come for her or leave. She was so anxious that she didn't even realise that he was gone until dinner time when she crept through to make them supper.

Earle rolled back in a little after midnight, reeking of moonshine and sex, his black suit as filthy as if he'd been rolling around in the gutters down by the docks. Mary didn't even dare to confront him. She knew that her Evan would have been too ashamed to come home in such a state, but this Earle? Who knew how he might react?

More and more often, Earle would just vanish while Mary was sleeping, and more and more, it was a source of profound relief for her. Some days he didn't bother to come home at all. Then it stretched out to a week. She did the unthinkable, taking herself down to the courthouse alone and airing all of the dirty laundry that she had sworn to herself that she would take to her grave in exchange for the divorce that she so sorely needed. The court issued a summons to Evan, to give evidence in his defence, but he failed to attend and the divorce proceedings dangled, unfinished without his input.

He never came by the home or troubled Mary ever again. It was as though he had forgotten that she ever existed. As if the whole time he had been Evan Fuller was just a dream that he had finally woken up from after his short sharp shock.

Earle Nelson was back on the streets of San Francisco, stalking and hunting for something he could not put a name to, the same restless energy that had always plagued him driving him on and on. When the sun rose high above the high tops of the buildings, he would scurry for the cover of darkness, telling whatever lies it took to slip out of sight.

Midday caught him on Pacific Avenue on May 19, 1921. His head had already been pounding to the sound of every footstep, but now old instincts screamed at him to seek out some deep dark place to shelter. Somewhere since abandoning his wife and home, he had exchanged his dour suit for a boiler suit like he wore when working in the hospital, though if you asked him how or when, he would not have been able to tell you. Just as he had never been able to tell his grandmother where the modest finery that she had garbed him in vanished to when he went roaming in the wilds.

It provided the perfect excuse for him to be indoors, however. He walked up to the door of 1519 Pacific Avenue and knocked on the door without a care in the world. When a young man answered, Earle gave him a smile and told him that he was a plumber, here to take a look at the boiler in their basement. Charles Summer Junior had no reason to distrust an adult. He'd never encountered a monster in men's clothing before. Inviting Earle in freely and directing him towards the basement, he went back to his own business without a second thought. If the man wasn't a plumber, then why would he possibly want to be in their basement in the middle of a gorgeous day?

Down in the dark, Earle felt like he could breathe easy at last. Nobody could see him; the judging light was not upon him. He could stay here all day, answering the questions that the angels posed him, reciting Revelations and basking in the peace. Down here far from sight, he could ignore the twisted, dark desires that had been shaken loose by his latest injury. The ones that he had fought so hard to crush back down into oblivion throughout his life, yet just wouldn't stop springing back up the moment his attention turned elsewhere. His head ached constantly, but instead of debilitating him, it now gave him clarity. Pain was an instrument of purification, and his mind was being purified by the fire within.

For a time, he thought that he had avoided his fate, the predestined end point of his life that he had foreseen back in his youth. He'd thought that he might live a normal life, with a normal wife, and be content the way that normal people were. He'd hoped that the furious lusts that had consumed him as a boy might be left behind when he had the outlet for them that the Bible told him were natural. Yet all through his marriage, his wife had rejected him and reviled him for acting out only the mildest of the fantasies that he had hoped to one day see fulfilled. Even when he did everything the way that the Lord and grandmother had told him to, he could not find any joy or satisfaction in it.

This second blow to the head had rattled him loose from his misconceptions. When he was a child, he had acted as a child, but now that he was a man, he needed to put aside childish things. First and foremost, he had to put aside the delusion that he was just like everyone else. He knew, even back when he was so small that he could barely recall it now, that the Lord spoke to him. Not only in the words of the angels and devils that whispered in his ears, but also in the way that the world reshaped itself around him. All too often, he had seen the path springing forth at his feet and leading him towards God's plan for him, and he had turned away because he wanted to play pretend. God guided him to the course that God wanted him to take, not by playing with Earle's thoughts and intentions, but by presenting him with opportunities.

When Mary, the twelve-year-old daughter of the Summers house, came wandering down the stairs into the basement, wondering who was talking down in the darkness, an opportunity presented itself. She did not know about the plumber. She did not know who this looming giant of a man was, grabbing her by the ankles and dragging her off into the darkness. She was too young and innocent to understand why he was trying to pull her clothes off; why he was grabbing onto the private parts of her body that nobody was ever meant to see or touch. All that she knew was that the bogeyman everyone had spent her whole life telling her was not lurking down in the basement was here, and he was trying to do something so horrible to her that she couldn't even put it in words. Mary screamed.

She screamed and screamed even as Earle tried to fumble a hand over her mouth and the buttons of his boiler suit out of place. She screamed and screamed, so loud that her brother, up two flights of stairs and at the other end of the household, heard her and came barrelling down to interrupt Earle before he could commit this new and most heinous act.

Earle looked up at Charles as though his eyes couldn't make him out in the dim. As though he could not believe that anyone else might be in the house even though they had passed one another just an hour before in the entryway. Charles was a little more worldly than his sister. He knew exactly what Earle was attempting, and he set about thrashing the man for it. A kick sent the lumbering ape of a man rolling off, but he was up again before there was a moment to regroup. Charles called out to his sister to run and fetch the police, but the sobbing child was still trying to pull her skirts back down.

That shout seemed to snap Earle out of his reverie, and he realised that whatever he'd believed was destined to happen down in that basement, it had now been brought to a halt. He had to escape. He tried to rush for the stairs, only to catch Charles's fist in his gut. It was not a fair fight as Earle wasn't even raising his hands to the young man, just trying to bull-rush through to freedom. Charles rained fury down on the thug. Kicking him, hitting him, and shoving him in equal measure. Mary scrambled up the stairs and ran out into the street, screaming for help. Yet her neighbours thought that it was just a child at play and paid her no heed.

By brute strength alone, Earle pushed his way back up the stairs, driving Charles through his home, step by agonising step. All the way out into the street. Out there Charles joined in his sister's screaming for help, and suddenly all eyes were turned their way. The scrutiny that Earle had struggled so hard to avoid throughout his lumbering life was now all turned his way. Everyone could see him. Everyone would know what he had done. That he was a sinner.

He tried to break and run, but Charles held onto his sleeve. Charles would not let the rapist run free to go after some other innocent child. He would not let this monster roam free.

Finally, Earle had the wherewithal to throw a punch, all of his brutal strength finally turned by panic to its purpose. The blow sent the young man flying. He was unconscious before he hit the ground.

Yet by now all of his neighbours had taken up the cries for the police, and they had rushed out to shield young Mary from the beast that had sought to do her harm. Faced down by a whole swarm of angry faces, Earle turned and fled.

He ran for his life from the furore that he had left behind, ducking down side streets and sprinting when there was nobody around to give him attention. A few neighbourhoods away, he climbed onto a streetcar and rode it to the end of the line, finally breathing easy, safe in the knowledge that he had escaped justice. The police were waiting for him at the street car depot.

Fast as Earle might have run, eyes were looking down on him from every window as news of the attack on a little girl spread. If the police hadn't caught up to Earle, then it was likely that the mothers of San Francisco, who were already out patrolling in force, would have beaten him to death with broom-handles. Earle's face was a mass of scratches from his brawl with Charles Summers. His boiler suit was ripped up so badly he'd dropped a sleeve without noticing. By the morning, when the police came back to take him before a judge, his appearance was even more odd. Through the night, he had been screaming at the faces in the wall for whispering lies to him, and with his fingernails, he had meticulously plucked every single hair from his eyebrows. The judge did not find Earle competent, so he was transferred immediately to a city hospital to undergo assessment.

It was here that Earle encountered his wife one final time. He did not recognise his visitor. He did not even acknowledge that she was there. For her part, she could hardly recognise him. After the stunt with his eyebrows, he was kept bound up in a straitjacket, confined to bed with thick leather straps. He reeked of his own filth, and he flung himself back and forth against his restraints, ranting and raving about the faces in the walls.

Mary wept when she saw the truth about her husband, and given this new information about his mental state and impending conviction, she had no trouble at all getting her divorce pushed through.

Yet even though she wanted no part of Earle's wicked world, she still could not leave him to his fate. She campaigned the court to treat him as a mental patient rather than a criminal, and so when sentencing came around, rather than being shipped off back to jail where he would likely have attempted to take his own life, Earle was instead committed once more to Napa State Hospital, a place that he had casually escaped so many times that it was almost laughable.

The notes on his condition from this time were a stark contrast to the gentle giant he had been framed as before. He was noted to be violent and dangerous to himself and others. Restless, apathetic, incendiary, depressed, Earle flicked back and forth between the extremes of his personality, with the only unifying factor seeming to be his religious mania.

He was diagnosed as a psychotic in the midst of an episode from the outset, but it would not take long before the staff added 'nomadic dementia' to his list of symptoms. He was obsessed with escaping from his confinement and travelling once more. Yet this time around, with the danger that Earle posed, there was none of the lackadaisical attitude that had allowed him to run free so often in the past. He was kept under lock and key, and during his limited exercise time in the gardens of the institution, he was kept shackled and bound.

Throughout his first year, Earle received daily treatments of Salversan – an anti-syphilis drug that seemed to bring his manic outbursts back under control. He became quiet, still talking about the blessings that were upon his doctors and quoting scripture as always, but no longer attempting to escape. He was granted more freedom, inch by inch, as it appeared his treatment was succeeding. He was allowed to complete menial tasks around the hospital, and it seemed that he might actually be on the road to recovery. Then the word 'quiet' disappeared from his weekly updates to be replaced with the word 'restless'. He began to refuse treatment and spoke once more about his intentions to escape.

On November 2, 1923, he made good on those intentions. When the orderlies were doing their rounds, they found that his bed was empty and had not been slept in. There was no sign of Earle anywhere, nor was there any indication of how he had managed to slip out.

Back in San Francisco, Lillian had almost entirely forgotten about her nephew. News of his divorce and incarceration had reached her, of course, but she had done all that she could to push her concerns for him aside. He may have been her flesh and blood, but he was in a better place now. Somewhere that might tend to his unique needs a little better than she could manage, keeping the boy locked away in her basement.

She was just about to take her children up to bed when she saw him.

He had on an oversized hat, stolen somewhere between Napa and there. It was pitch black behind him, so the only thing to be seen through the window was his pale face, illuminated by the light from inside the house. In the dim light, his bugged-out eyes were black. His expression contorted into a caricature artist's impression of a madman. The children screamed and fled to their mother. Lillian herself was shaken at the sight of Earle, but still he was her flesh and blood. She could not turn her back on him, no matter what occurred. Dragging the children every step of the way, Lillian walked over to the front door and unlocked it.

The gentle giant of yesteryear was well and truly gone. Earle had gone from being soft in the head to being viscerally dangerous in only a few short years. Where before Lillian would have embraced her nephew, regardless of the state that he was in, now she was too frightened to even approach him. She went through all the motions of supporting him, fetching one of her husband's suits for him to wear and warning him that he had to get out of town as this was the first place that they would come looking for him. But in truth, she did not want this man in her house. She could not be rid of him fast enough.

The moment that he was out in the streets once more, Lillian got on the phone to first the police, then to Napa Hospital, giving them Earle's location, a description of his new disguise, and an entreaty to find him soon before he came back. She feared what he might do.

It took two more days before the police and Napa staff managed to track Earle down. Two days in which he could have been committing all manner of atrocities. As luck would have it, all that he had spent the time doing was roaming the streets of San Francisco aimlessly. Like he was a tourist.

His feet were blistered and his borrowed clothes in tatters by the time that he was brought back to Napa and stripped down. That was when the kid gloves came off. If Earle was going to be a naughty boy, running away, then he was going to be treated like a naughty boy. There was no sponge bath waiting for him once he'd shucked his borrowed suit. Only the hydrotherapy hose. There were no comfortable bed, books, or flowers in his new room. Only a bare cot. They had tried being gentle with Earle, and the result had been betrayal. They had spared the rod and spoiled the child. All official records of the 'treatment' that Earle received from that point forward have either been destroyed or notation stopped. Needless to say, it must have been brutal if even the doctors of the 1920s thought it was too grim to write about.

Sixteen more months passed following his recapture, then abruptly he was cut loose, with his records. It had been four years to the day since his attack on Mary Summers. May 19, 1925.

So That All May See Your Progress

Clara Newman was a frail woman of sixty years. Yet time had done nothing to soften her sharp business acumen. If anything, experience had given her an edge over the other landlords that she encountered. She firmly believed herself to be a good judge of character, capable of sniffing out a charlatan before he had a hope of turning her head. She maintained large landholdings back on the East Coast while also running a plethora of boarding houses around the Bay Area. She stayed in the house at 2037 Pierce Street, along with her nephew and his family, albeit in different studio apartments.

On February 20, 1926, she was in the midst of cooking herself a sausage for lunch when she heard a rapping on the front door. All of her residents had their own keys, so she was puzzled until she recalled the 'Room for Rent' sign that she had posted in the window. Turning off the heat under the pan, she headed to the door to find out what was happening.

Roger Wilson was there waiting for her, dark of clothing and so deeply tanned she wondered at his parentage. Despite his rather grim appearance, he introduced himself politely in a soft-spoken voice and enquired if the room was still available to rent. He may have been a hulking man, but the book grasped in his massive hand was unmistakeably the Good one. Clara decided to hear him out and see if her rules about lady visitors and drinking would be adhered to.

Earle had no hesitation or thought for the other residents of the large building. The moment that they were in the receiving room, he lunged forwards, wrapping those massive hands around Clara's throat and bearing her to the ground. She could not scream. He had learned from young Mary Summer the dangers of a scream. He had learned from his own Mary that even an unconscious body could serve his purposes when he needed release. In fact, it would be more pliant than any whore. She writhed beneath him, as she tried to scramble away, but it was to no avail. She had neither the strength nor the leverage to overpower Earle. She slipped into darkness. Given what would come next, that was probably a kindness.

Suddenly aware of how exposed he was, and how difficult it had been to escape from a basement the last time he had attempted something like this, Earle picked Clara up by the neck and carried her like a sack of potatoes up the stairs to the apartment for rent. Judging that carefully dusted but otherwise undisturbed place to be a closet where he would likely find privacy, Earle pushed Clara's skirts up the rest of the way and mounted her with an animal grunt.

Once he had taken his pleasure with the old woman's dead body, he tidied himself up and headed down the stairs and was almost out of the door before he was stopped in his tracks by somebody calling out. 'Can I help you, sir?'

Earle did not look back. For the first time in a long time, his mind was missing its characteristic pain and fog. He spoke clear as day. 'Please tell the landlady that I shall take the room. I will return in an hour.'

The man left a moment later, leaving Merton Newman more confused than before. Merton had come down from his chilled apartment to check on the boiler in the basement when he noticed that his aunt was missing from her accustomed place in the kitchen. The partly cooked sausage was still there on the stovetop, so she could not have gone far. He half expected to run into her down in the basement where he gave the boiler a jolly good kicking. On his way back up, he paused in the hallway to greet this dark stranger and receive his curious statement. He passed through into the receiving room to peer out after the stranger, only to realise that he had entirely vanished from sight already. It was an oddity, but one that the practical man set aside. He had bookkeeping tasks to attend to in his apartment.

An hour or so later, with his work complete, Merton came back down to ask his aunt about the new tenant only to find the kitchen in the same state of disarray. The fat in the pan had now congealed, but nothing else had changed. Perplexed more than worried, Merton began searching for Aunt Clara throughout the building, enlisting the other neighbours as he encountered them until finally, just as his wife and children were returning from the matinee at the local cinema that had granted him his peace and quiet to finish up his work, somebody thought to check in the empty space.

Clara was still lying there on the floor of the unlet boarding room, her exposed legs splayed out like a whore's, her cooling body turning grey and rich dark bruises already blossoming around her throat. Merton was sick. The police were summoned. The newspapers reported on the crime, but the gruesome details of necrophilia were not printed, for obvious reasons. It was a grim event, but not one that attracted much attention.

It seemed to Earle that if God had not wanted that woman to die, she would not have invited him in. It seemed to him that if God wanted him to stop, then the police would have caught him. All of his other crimes and sins had been instantly punished. The world had always shifted to keep him on the course that it wanted. Now, suddenly, he found that he could kill without compunction or fear of vengeance. The truth was that God wanted him to kill. God gave him his lusts, and his strength, and hid him from the sight of man so that he could do this work. He did not know why the Lord sought the death of these women or rewarded him with such pleasure for it. He did not know if he was the Great Beast, awoken from the pit as Revelations prophesied, or merely a man sinning so that others would be driven to the righteous path. He could not know any of these things, for as he had been taught since birth the Lord moved in mysterious ways. The Lord moved him in mysterious ways.

It took two weeks before the Lord moved him again, during which time less divine criminal instincts drove him out of the city of San Francisco and off into California, all the way to San Jose. On March 2, he felt the same call that he had when looking up at Clara's 'Room for Rent' sign. The same divine inspiration, when all of the chaos that usually stormed behind his eyes suddenly cleared and granted him the clarity that he needed to not only act but to act with complete and utter precision. Just as he could never recall where he had found his clothes, so too were his current accompaniments and accessories a puzzle to him. He did not know where he had acquired a black suit, a hat, a Bible, or a suitcase. Yet he had them and carried them with him on his way up to the door of the house.

Laura Beale was sixty-three years old and still happily married to a local estate agent. This time, Earle's lies came more readily and easily. They were practised, and he did not have to pause and ponder each answer for so long that it brought the whole thing to a crashing halt. He continued to learn from his mistakes, asking for Laura to show him the room that was to let before laying his hands on her, and even then, only covering her mouth rather than choking the life out of her. How could he choke her when she wouldn't lift her head up high enough for him to get under her chin? He bore her to the ground and tore at her clothes. Wrestling and struggling. Tugging and ripping. The silk belt of her house-coat tore free of its stitching and he tied it around her neck in a great loop, pulling on either end of it while she bucked and choked beneath him. He did not need a fraction of his strength with a garotte, but still he brought it all to bear. Pulling and pulling until the silk cord cut through her skin and into her flesh. Blood streaked down her neck. Pulsing out in time to her terrified heartbeat. If he had not been distracted by the heaving of her body beneath him and turned his attention to other pleasures, it was likely he would have gone on tightening that noose until she was decapitated entirely.

The blood slowed and stopped. The struggling came to a halt. She was dead. A still doll version of a living woman, one that he could pose and use as he saw fit. There was no judgement from her, so Earle felt that he was committing no sin. As he shucked off her undergarments, he felt no guilt about studying her wrinkled flesh. Sniffing at the air. Pawing at her private places. Dead, she could not hurt him. Dead, she could not shame him. With the strength of his hands he had stolen her power. Now Grandma could not cast him aside when it suited her. Now she could not condemn him to confinement or darkness. She was all for him. Not aunties and uncles or strangers. Him and him alone.

When Laura's husband returned home from work, he was mystified to discover that his wife was missing. At her age, Laura very rarely left the house alone, and she certainly never did so unannounced. Many of the marginally younger women who boarded in the house would have been happy to accompany her if she had needed to pop out for something, yet not one of them had heard a peep from Laura all day.

A search of the building turned up no sign of her until the empty apartment was discovered to have been left unlocked. One of the elderly women entered first and then fainted right away. Mr Beale darted forward to catch the old woman only to catch sight of his wife and lose his grip entirely. It fell to a neighbour to fetch the police. The residents were all too distraught.

Examination of the body revealed another post-mortem rape had occurred, and the San Jose Police immediately linked this slaughter with Clara Newman's death. A call went out for witnesses, but apart from Merton Newman's description of 'a dark giant of a man', the only sighting of anyone suspicious near to the Beale boarding house was of a sallow-faced man with no distinguishing characteristics noted.

When Earle saw the news in the local paper connecting his two crimes, it became clear to him that the anonymity that distance had always granted him would no longer suffice. Before, he had been able to run from his problems with ease, hopping from one jurisdiction to the next without fear of pursuit. He had to rely on God to protect him now.

With all thoughts of geography and worldly avoidance of the law set aside, Earle allowed his feet to lead him, hopping the first box-train back to San Francisco, passing invisibly by the police lurking around the station trying to spot anyone who matched his description by bypassing the actual station entirely.

For a solid month, stories of the 'Dark Strangler' circulated in the local papers, describing an almost spectral figure that could slip into women's homes unnoticed. These stories were printed alongside increasingly cartoonish depictions of a sallow-faced man with arms so long his knuckles trailed the ground. The Dark Strangler graduated from being a criminal menace feared by all to an almost folkloric figure discussed in the same breath as Paul Bunyan. By the end of that month, the truth had been entirely forgotten, and the very real danger had been discarded along with all the jokes and rumours as the news moved on to the next big thing.

Earle felt safe to pick up a daily paper once more, ignoring all the news of the day to peruse the classified section, where the boarding houses with rooms to let were listed out. It was the end of March 1928 before he replied to another advert.

Lillian St. Mary was a destitute widow with an adult son still living at home. In desperation, she had turned to renting out rooms to boarders to supplement a pension that could barely stretch to essentials. The accommodations were less than stellar. Lillian was sixty-three years old, her eyesight was failing her, and she was frail. As a result, the house was clogged with dust from top to bottom, and her layabout son did nothing to help in the upkeep. As a result of the unhygienic conditions, renters had been few and far between, and the majority of her empty rooms remained so.

She was heading out to collect her pension when she was startled by a figure looming on her doorstep, his hand upraised to knock. Few words were exchanged on that step, with Earle simply stating that he was interested in renting a room. Lillian was so overjoyed at the prospect that she forgot all propriety and immediately invited him up to see what she had available. She was so lost in the excitement of potentially having an income that she didn't even pause to strip off her overcoat before leading him through.

As they ascended the stairs, Earle rambled on through his prepared story. Even though Lillian hadn't shown the first hint of suspicion or interest, he still pushed on through it diligently. He was new to the Bay Area. He wanted to rent someplace cheap as he was saving up to get married. Lillian swept ahead of him into a second-floor room, explaining weekly rent, dinner time, and the situation with towels as she went. Both of them entirely lost in their own little fantasy of how the interaction was playing out. The click of the lock snapped them both back to reality.

His hands were around her throat before she could even ask what he thought he was doing. He bore her down to the ground, then sat on her chest, getting comfortable while he squeezed the life out of her. The little air she had in her lungs was crushed out of her by his weight. She writhed and strained beneath him, but he was so much larger and stronger than her that he barely seemed to notice. In one smooth movement, he had taken her from standing to the precipice of unconsciousness beneath him. It had been so swift that the glasses had not even been displaced from her nose.

Behind those thick lenses, Earle watched Lillian's eyes grow bloodshot. He watched as they bulged out of her skull as the pressure inside her head increased. Blood was still frantically pumping in, trying to keep her brain alive, but he was squeezing too tightly for any to escape. Her eyes bulged and bulged until they were almost touching the slices of glass, then suddenly, all too suddenly, everything stopped. He could not feel the pulse of life beneath his crushing fingers. He could not feel the feeble attempts of this body to push him off. As fast as he had taken a hold of her, death had followed all the more swiftly.

With care, he stripped off her overcoat and folded it neatly. With care, he lifted her up and laid her on the neatly made bed of the room. With abandon, he rucked up her skirts and climbed between her legs, mouth and hands roaming across skin that was never meant to be seen, let alone touched. She had not made a sound as he murdered her, and she did not make a sound now as he violated her dead body, over and over. In the stuffy dusty silence of the empty room, the only noise was Earle. His rough breathing, his grunts, his moans, his recitation of scripture to justify his evil.

When he was done, he placed her folded coat up on the bed between her spread-eagled feet. He retrieved her hat from where it had fallen and added it on top of that heap. Without another word, he left the way that he had come, unlocking the door and strolling down the stairs and into the street with a grin on his face. A streetcar conductor caught a glimpse of him as he wandered away, and the image of that sallow face was burned into his memory.

Lillian's body was discovered by one of her tenants later in the day. He noticed that the door to the empty room sat ajar and stuck his head inside to see if he had a new neighbour. He spotted Lillian on the bed before he had time to even call out, and he left immediately to seek out the police, running down the stairs with such a commotion that it bothered the tenant from the apartment below where the murder and rape had been committed - a man who had not heard a single sound throughout the day.

If the Dark Strangler had been a myth before, now he graduated to a full-blown nightmare for the San Francisco police as well as anyone trying to rent out a room. A long list of warnings was printed in the papers, warning women not to show rooms alone and to be wary of any strange man that approached them regardless of how closely he resembled their imaginings about the monstrous strangler. The police believed that they had a murderous madman on their hands, and that by their nature, madmen were incapable of covering their tracks. This imbecile would come out from under his rock before too long, make another attempt on a woman, and be caught, thanks to the safety precautions that they were suggesting. It would be just a matter of time before he was off the streets, according to the Chief of Police.

The whole city was on high alert, just waiting for this monster to jump out at them, yet nothing happened. A month passed and there was no sign of the Dark Strangler. Some rumours had begun to circulate, pushing him even further into the realms of fantasy. An offhand quip about his not even being a man, but rather an escaped gorilla from a travelling zoo, transformed public opinion of him from a bogeyman to a laughingstock, his victims into punchlines.

Stories in the papers adopted this new joke as part of their coverage. Earle became the 'Gorilla Man' or 'Gorilla Killer' in their headlines. Another month passed, and he slipped even further from the minds of the general populace. Not even a joke anymore, he was forgotten.

I Will Fear No Evil

Santa Barbara was a world away from the hustle and bustle of the big city. It was a town in its own right, with a blossoming population, but none of the wickedness that seemed to afflict other places had spread there. It was a place where folks still felt safe to leave their doors unlocked at night, even if there was a huge transient population moving through. Santa Barbara had become the gateway to Southern California, and all the itinerant farm workers seeking out seasonal work there had to pass through this town on the way. It brought a steady influx of wealth to the otherwise docile community, transforming it into a resort town of sorts, and had resulted in a burgeoning industry for hostels, hotels, and boarding houses.

So far from San Francisco, the locals had heard tell of the Gorilla Killer, but none of them ever believed that he might darken their door. Bad things might happen in big cities full of sin and debauchery, but here in Santa Barbara? It seemed ridiculous.

Will Franey was one of the long-term residents in Mrs Ollie Russell's boarding house. With the odd hours that he was required to keep as a railroad worker, the living situation suited him well. He could sleep there through the day or the night without the risk of interruption, as Mr and Mrs Russell ran a tight ship, coming down hard on anyone disrupting their peace.

He came home from his regular shift as the sun was rising, walking through the silent town and the empty streets, already halfway to sleep. He let himself into the house and slipped silently through the halls, feet guided by muscle memory to avoid the creaky floorboards. His key turned in the well-oiled lock of his door and his eyes were already closed. The outer layers of his work-wear fell away from him, crusted with dust and oil, and he collapsed face-first into the bed.

Exhaustion carried him down into the dark and held him there for a few hours, but it wasn't nearly long enough. Knocking. Someone was knocking. His eyes felt like they were crusted shut, but with a strain of effort, he opened them to the sunlight streaming in narrow beams through his moth-eaten curtains. He groaned. Who was knocking? Everyone knew his shifts. Why hadn't Mrs Russell dealt with any callers? Still halfway to sleep, he rose up and fumbled into a pair of trousers, trying and failing three times to get the suspenders untangled and over his shoulders before giving up. Tripping over yesterday's clothes, he made it to the door and let his head rest against the cool wood.

Bending a little, he forced an eye open to peer through the peephole. There was nobody in the hall. He leaned back, his sleep-addled brain creaking as it tried to comprehend the conflicting information. There was nobody at his door, but somebody was still knocking. Hard and rhythmic. Non-stop.

It took him longer than he'd like to admit to realise that the knocking was on his wall, not his door. The banging was coming from the room next door.

Still wrestling with his braces, Will lumbered out into the hallway and stomped along to the next door, ready to give whoever was there a good telling off. Once more his barely conscious brain was struggling to fill in details. Who lived in this room? Wasn't it empty?

Puzzled by his inability to recall, he hunched down and peered through the keyhole to jog his memory. There was a man in a dark suit looming over the bed. He was moving back and forth. Banging the headboard against the wall to create that infernal knocking. A dark tanned man that Will didn't recognise. Was this a new tenant?

Will blinked away his confusion and put his eye to the keyhole once more. There was a woman on the bed. He couldn't see her face, but he could see the bare length of a thigh propped up against the dark fabric of the man's suit. Even now it took Will a moment to put it all together. Sex. The banging was the headboard of the bed on his wall. This strange man and woman were having sex up against his wall and stirring him from his sleep. Will flushed, mortified, and backed all the way into his room. He couldn't believe what he'd just seen. There was no way that Mrs Russell would approve of something like that happening under her roof. Will hadn't even been allowed to entertain his girl cousin in the common room without Ollie and her husband there to serve as chaperones.

He should go and tell her. He should go and warn her about the disreputable things happening under her roof. But first, he needed to find out who was doing the disreputable thing up against his wall. He hadn't recognised the man, which meant it must have been one of the lady tenants. If it was one of the lady tenants, he certainly couldn't recognise them just by the sight of their bare legs. He'd have to go back and crouch down to look through the keyhole again until he could get a proper look at her, naked and spread out on the bed for some strange man. It wasn't prurient interest. He didn't want to see naked women. It was just an unfortunate side effect of identifying which one of the unwed ladies in the house was easy with her affections. Identifying her for the purpose of reporting her, of course. Definitely not so that he could approach her later.

He crept back into the hall, doing his best to stay silent this time around, not that anyone would hear a thing over that infernal thumping and knocking. He brought his eye to the keyhole again and he stared. There was the man, hat still on his head. There was the glimpse of thigh, the leg flopping around. White lace socks told Will nothing. The skirts had all been pushed up around this woman's waist, but he could make out the colours if not the details. It was a patterned dress in navy with a paler blue patterning. The same colours that he could have sworn he'd seen Mrs Russell wearing every other day of the week. That gave him pause. The more he looked, the more he could make out the wrinkles on this woman's legs, the varicose veins running up her calves. He pulled back from the door.

It couldn't possibly be her. She was a married woman. A married woman obsessed with propriety. She couldn't possibly be having an extramarital affair. He stared in again, desperately trying to see her face, to prove to himself that the Ollie Russell he knew would never do such a thing. His eyes proved him a liar. He had no doubt in his mind after watching for a few more minutes that this was definitely his landlady, giving herself over to animal lusts with some ravening beast of a man.

The stirrings that Will had felt when he'd realised what was happening in the next room had now been replaced with a sickly feeling in his stomach. He returned to his room and locked the door. He couldn't believe what he had seen, and he wanted to escape from the social nightmare that it had placed him in. He could not bring himself to disrobe, laying back on his unmade bed to stare up at the ceiling and realise that sleep would not be an escape. The thumping went on and on. Hammering the images into his head. He felt sick. Every beat on the wall was another nail in the coffin of his mental health. Will lay there listening against his will to every thump and bump. Until finally, blessedly, the hammering on his wall ceased and he was able to breathe again. In the silence that ensued, he could swear that he could hear everything. The shuffling of feet. The creaking of the door. The heavy steps in the hall, making every one of the floorboards sing. The man was right outside of Will's door. All that he'd have to do was walk over and put his eye to the peephole to know his face, but Will didn't want to know. He didn't want any more of the sordid details. He didn't want any part in this desecration of the holy ground of his home. How could he look Ollie in the eye now, having seen her sin? How could he tolerate this knowledge?

He rose. Nausea gurgling in his gut. This was wrong. Dressing himself, he walked back to the door of the room where it happened. He tried the door, but it was locked. To his shame, Will was relieved. He did not need to confront the jezebel in her lair. He looked back through the keyhole. The woman remained unmoving on the bed. Uncovered now that her lover had departed. Her face was turned away, but now she was unmistakable. All of Will's wilful ignorance of the situation fell away in an instant. That was Ollie, but the whole story was still unfolding in front of his eyes. There was red around her throat. Red on the bedcovers. Something was even more wrong than he had thought.

The only person with a key to the room, other than Ollie, was her husband. So Will sought the man out, bringing him home from the store and standing by as the key turned in the lock.

When the police arrived, they took note of the blood smeared on the doorframe. The blood soaked into the mattress. The ruined and beaten face of Ollie Russell, so swollen and discoloured that she could not be recognised. The blood, all that blood, had come from the wound on her neck. A cord pulled tight enough to tear her flesh apart as it choked the breath out of her.

The sickness finally took over Will as he stood by, listening to all of this and giving his statement. Ollie had already been dead when he saw her desecration. He had been lying in his bed, listening to the corpse of his close acquaintance being raped. He rushed off to the shared bathroom to empty his guts.

Will's testimony proved next to useless. If he had looked through his peephole as the killer passed, he might have been able to bring the man to justice. As it was, his eye-witness account provided nothing but colour to the news stories circulated around America in the coming days.

The police in Santa Barbara were not as worldly or circumspect as their cousins in the big city. News of the necrophilia began to spread around, and the legend of the Gorilla Killer transformed once more into something far more sickening. A nightmare that haunted the nights of the West Coast, every one of them just waiting for the Gorilla Killer to strike again. The whole world waited with bated breath.

On August 16, 1926, Oakland was hot. Across the bay from San Francisco, they usually enjoyed much the same temperate weather, thanks to the breeze off the water, but not that year. It was as though the doors of Hell had been left hanging open in some dark alley, and the oppressive heat had the whole town on edge.

Stephen Nisbet came home from work already tense. The late summer heat and humidity were making him miserable, and he could not keep his mind focused on the task at hand. It kept drifting like he was lulled halfway into a dream by the damned heat, slipping into fantasies and nightmares. When he stepped into the boarding house, none of the usual spring was in his step, and when he came to the kitchen and found a meal halfway through preparation, he felt anxiety beginning to gnaw at him. A quick check confirmed that his wife Mary had left her purse in the bedroom. She would not have gone out without it. He settled himself at the kitchen table to wait for her to appear, setting his watch down in front of him so that he could count the minutes down. After an hour had elapsed, his attempts to distract himself from his suspicions utterly failed, and he enlisted the other men of the house to help search for her, already fearing the worst. This close to San Francisco, he was all too familiar with tales of the Gorilla Killer. In his mind, he had played out this nightmare scenario so many times already that it almost felt familiar when he opened up the unoccupied second floor room and saw that the bathroom door was hanging ajar.

He could not look. He could not walk willingly into the nightmare. He could already see blood on the tiles and a glimpse of his wife's pale flesh, twisted and contorted to fit down the side of a toilet. It was already clear to him what had happened, so with tears in his eyes, he went out to fetch the police.

It was for the best that he did not enter the bathroom. The policemen who did, to record the scene of the crime, emerged pale and queasy. The dishtowel that Mary habitually kept draped over her shoulder had been tied around her neck and pulled until it ripped apart, but even that was not the limit of the atrocities on display. Her head had been slammed into the walls and floor of the bathroom with such force that every tooth in her mouth had been knocked out. They lay scattered across the floor amidst the smears of blood. The blood itself was everywhere. Splattered across the fixtures and up the walls. The biggest pool was, of course, down the side of the toilet itself, where the broken and raped body of Mary Nisbet had been stuffed with such force that both of her hip joints and shoulders were dislocated.

The police immediately took Stephen into custody. This was clearly a crime of passion, and who could have any passion for a fifty-year-old housewife other than her husband? They questioned him over and over for a gruelling forty hours as the real killer slipped out of town entirely unnoticed.

By the time that the police bothered to check his alibi and confirm that Stephen had been at work during the horrific events in his own home, Earle himself had moved on across the state line, his black suit still looking immaculate despite his being able to feel the dampness of blood upon it. The Bible was still clasped in his hand, and Revelations on his lips.

The Trinity

Earle travelled north, jumping trains where he could but buying his own ticket just as often. He passed unseen through the other travellers, ignored or unimportant to everyone else in the world. The Lord still protected him and held him close to His heart. This he knew. There could be no resurrection without revelation. There could be no victory without the battle on the fields of Armageddon. War is the great day of God Almighty. He needed a Great Beast to rise up and sound the trumpet. All of these women, so like his grandmother and his wife in their purity and certainty of faith, they had to die. He had to do the things that he did, for if he did no evil, then there could be no good. It was so obvious now why he had been set on this course, why his whole life had forged him into a weapon, a tool in the hand of the Lord.

On October 19, 1926, Beata Withers went missing from her boarding house in Portland, Oregon. The next day, Virginia Grant disappeared during a visit to a property she owned on East 22nd Street. The day after that, Mabel Fluke disappeared from her home. Three days, and three women. The last had already been taken before the body of the first was uncovered. Beata Withers was only 35, considerably younger than the majority of Earle's victims and quite young for a landlady at that. She had a fifteen-year-old son living with her who would tend to the jobs around the property that needed a man's touch. He was surprised by her youth. It shook him out of the fantasy that he had been replaying over and over in his head. This was not the stern mother figure whom he had to punish for her transgressions against him. This was not the kind of woman who would try to control him. She was something else, and he could not understand why God had brought him to her door. Not until she turned her head in that certain way that made a curl of her hair fall down onto her forehead, and he instantly knew her as his Aunt Lillian. The very first object of his lusts. The very first thing that had been denied to him. He killed her. He raped her. All was as he had wanted it to be all those years ago as he watched her undress.

Forbidden lusts were fulfilled. His sister and his aunt and his caretaker all in one. Yet when he was done with her, he felt something he had not anticipated. Shame burned in him. She had seen him. Her eyes had lulled open in the violence of his motions. She'd seen him doing the dirty things that he'd done. He had to hide. He had to hide the evidence.

Before, he'd felt no compulsion to do much of anything with the bodies. His grandmother deserved whatever she got, and her facsimiles the same. He'd tidied them out of the way when they were inconveniencing him, but for the most part, he'd left them where they lay. Yet this Lillian, she deserved his kindness. She'd been so good to him, and this was how he'd repaid her. Carrying her up into the attic, he emptied some clothes out of a steamer trunk and carefully folded her body inside, returning what he'd removed to cover her. Now nobody would see her shame. Nobody would know the filthy thing she'd done. She could rest in peace.

Virginia Grant did not receive the same sort of kindness. In the empty house that she was trying to rent out to this dark stranger, there was no need for restraint or shame - there was no need even to muffle her voice by choking the life out of her - yet old habits die hard. He tricked her into tilting back her head by asking about a mark on the ceiling, then caught her before she could speak another word. He was a master of his art now. Well-versed in murder, and an expert in his methodology. He killed her. He raped her. He was readying himself to leave when he felt another prickle in his mind. Not of conscience exactly, more like the nagging feeling of a task left only partially completed. Her body still lay on the floor of the house. It was untidy. Cleanliness was next to godliness. Grandmother had taught him that.

There was no handy coffin stowed away in the closets or the attics, and in the dark of the basement, where usually he felt the safest, Earle found only a substantial old boiler clunking away. He stuffed the corpse down behind it and was satisfied. As for Mabel Fluke, there was no sign of her at all. Fears for her safety began the moment that she went missing and only continued to worsen as each of the other women in Portland was discovered, one after another. The public knew that the Dark Strangler was among them. They knew that he was killing these women. Yet still the police refused to issue any statement connecting the missing women with the ones down in California. If they admitted that the Strangler was there, he became their problem. They did not want that kind of trouble.

Before the third body could turn up, a jury was assembled to examine the coroner's findings of Virginia Grant. From the body alone, there was ambiguity about the cause of death. Despite her body having been forcibly stuffed into a gap between a brick wall and a boiler, the actual cause of death appeared to be asphyxiation by hanging; Earle's assaults were so violent that he could crack bones as easily as a gallows.

This being the case, the coroner had concluded that Grant might have committed suicide rather than being killed by some monstrous killer. Immense political pressure was brought to bear on the citizens involved in this six-person jury, but even with all of the favours being exchanged and threats being made, it ended up hung with three believing that Grant had been murdered and the other three insisting that she might have killed herself and then stuffed herself down the side of her boiler.

This was enough ambiguity for Portland's police department to declare the case unproven. The longer they could delay, the more likely it was that the whole thing would pass out of the public's memory and they could return to business as usual. The rape of Grant's corpse was passed off by the pressured coroner to be possible evidence of sexual activity prior to death rather than a clear sign that her dead body had been interfered with, and the jury members studying the evidence were too sheltered to even consider the possibility of necrophilia. Earle was literally too evil for them to conceive of his actions.

It wasn't until days later that Mabel Fluke was finally discovered, not because the search had continued, but because of the smell. Residents in her boarding house already had their suspicions that Mabel had never left the building, and as the days rolled on, the aroma of decay grew alongside their concerns. Eventually, one brave soul explored the crawl space in the attic and discovered her corpse stuffed into the eaves of the building. The police were called in and retrieved her remains in rotten pieces. Despite all of their best attempts at obfuscation, there could be no doubt now that the Gorilla Killer had come to Portland. Fear stalked the streets, and the public screamed to their elected officials for action.

Forced out of their complacency, the police finally stepped up to the plate and began their investigation. By the time that they began asking questions, Earle had already departed, but that did not mean their efforts were fruitless.

Descriptions of the mysterious smiling man from each crime scene were collated, and outreach to the local community began to pay dividends. Earle's invisibility had faltered in this smaller town. He was an odd-looking stranger in neighbourhoods where everyone knew each other. It wasn't difficult to trace his wanderings back to their source. His barber was discovered. The boy who polished his shoes for a nickel. The pawn shop where he had traded valuables for the cash he used to pay his way. Every new piece of information brought the police closer to the Gorilla Killer's true identity.

The actual boarding house where he had resided in Portland was discovered, so like the scenes of his murders yet inexplicably passed over for the chaos that he usually sowed. Earle himself may have departed, but the false name that he had given when making his rental remained behind him, and it was simple enough to ask around about that alias, both in the town and beyond. It was recognised, time and again, by prostitutes down in San Francisco and by police in the little California ranch towns that he had once frequented. The alias of Mr Woodcox was known, and using that to track back to his point of origin, the Portland Police managed to identify Earle Nelson of San Francisco as the Gorilla Killer and publish his name and face in every paper in the country.

The press swarmed his aunt and uncle for information, and so his whole sordid history passed into the public domain. Stories of his bestial feeding habits and feats of acrobatics only served to heighten the feeling that he was more animal than human. That he truly was a great ape given human form.

Lillian was the one who knew the most of Earle's history up until this point, as he changed identities as readily as his clothes, yet even her accounts of him were incomplete. He had lived so long in solitude, passing invisibly from place to place, from life to life, that the press and later biographers had no hope of putting together the full picture. Yet from her, fragments were withdrawn that could later be expanded. Lillian did not speak of Earle's sexual obsession with her and her mother, yet these things became public knowledge after old school friends were bribed to part with their stories. When his now ex-wife was discovered, the press hounded her until she, too, had to vanish, but not before sharing stories of his bizarre sexual appetites, his obsession with older women, his insistence on behaving like a petulant child, and her observations of him within the sanitorium where he had been confined.

His medical history could not be officially divulged, yet all of the staff that no longer worked in the hospitals where he had been confined through the years were more than happy to share their horror stories about him. About the Great Beast of Revelations that he presumed himself to be.

Yet through all of this media furore, Earle remained invisible. While the police kept watch at every train station, it was as though he was moving through some invisible world. In a sense, he was. The civilised world knew nothing about the rail-riding underworld of the homeless and the hobos.

There was a whole subculture of itinerant people in 1920s America, and the trains were the thing that joined them all together. Petty criminals, homosexuals, travelling farm workers, paederasts, ethnic minorities, and the mentally ill all kept each other company in box cars across the states, and more importantly, they all protected one another from the law. Even if they knew that the Gorilla Killer was among them, they would not have turned him over to the enemy of the itinerant. After all, there was no greater enemy to the homeless than a landlord, and those were the ones that the Dark Strangler targeted.

God may have protected Earle. The hobos may have protected him. The whole setup of 1920s society, where every different city and state was its own little fiefdom refusing to communicate with one another, protected him, too. He was invisible, untouchable, and his crusade pressed on.

A Sojourner on the Earth

With him always moving, there was no way for the police to predict where Earle would strike next, and try as they might to instil a healthy fear of him into the populace, there just wasn't enough time for the majority of them to even grasp what was happening. The fact that he now struck without warning did nothing to help direct the manhunt or to provide those most in danger from him the appropriate forewarning.

Back in San Francisco, a city that the police swore blind that Earle would never dare to set foot in again, William Edmonds returned home on November 18th to discover his wife of thirty-five years, Anna, had been strangled to death with a twisted rag and raped in their marital bed after making the mistake of showing their spare room to a potential lodger.

It was clearly the work of Earle Nelson, but nobody could believe he had come and gone from the city without attracting any attention. They couldn't believe that anyone would go somewhere so dangerous to their own wellbeing. They did not understand yet that sanity was not a feature in his makeup.

He might have worn it as a mask, just as he did his piety, but neither one was truly him. The forces that guided him were not the same as the ones that drove a rational man to action. He heard the voices of angels and demons whispering him guidance. He sought answers in the Bible to questions that were all too worldly, flicking to a random page and using it like a toy for fortune telling instead of seeking moral guidance. The very next day, on the 19th of November, Earle struck again, just a short distance around the bay, in the town of Burlingame, a peaceful place full of eucalyptus groves and sea breezes, untouched by the corruption of their neighbouring city, as far as they knew.

Mrs H Murray had a home for sale at 1114 Grove Avenue, and an interested buyer had sent a telegram requesting a viewing that very day. She greeted the buyer when she arrived at the house and found him waiting but found nothing objectionable about him. If anything, he seemed rather a quiet and polite gentleman. Presumably because of his size, he had sidestepped the boisterousness that often passed for personality among the upper set. She did note a rather unpleasant aroma around the man, but she had too much class to comment upon such things.

Within the house, he became animated, commenting extensively upon architectural features that Mrs Murray herself had never even considered, and excitedly asking for information that only a serious buyer would request. For instance, he very badly wanted for her to take him down into the dark of the basement and show him the boiler. If he was to live here, he would need to know that his heating needs could be met.

Mrs Murray explained that she could not risk the stairs down into the basement herself due to being quite heavily pregnant at the time, but she was certain that her husband might be available to give him a more thorough tour once he was off work.

Thwarted in his attempts to go down into the dark, Earle instead turned his eyes to the heavens, exclaiming about the quality of the cornice work done around the ceiling in the hallway. This bait Mrs Murray took, looking up.

In an instant he was upon her, fingers tightening around her throat. She fought him. She struggled to scream. She wept and pled for the life of her baby boy, still inside her. Earle froze. Mrs Murray was barely twenty-five years old, and now he could not see an object for his pleasure spread upon the stairs beneath him - he could see his mother. She would have been about this age when she died. Leaving her little boy alone in the world. Earle was no sadist. He did not want to cause the kind of pain that he had suffered. He was simply fulfilling the directive given to him by God through his innate impulses. His grip loosened, and Mrs Murray was able to scramble back up the stairs away from him, screaming all the way. By the time that she'd recovered enough to stagger to her feet and run out in search of the police, the Dark Strangler was gone. Vanished once more into whatever shadow world he dwelled in between his slaughters.

Four days passed with the whole of California in a panic. The story of Mrs Murray had spread like wildfire along with an updated description of Earle, including even more incendiary details about his supposed physical deformities and dark appearance. Everyone in the state was jumping at shadows, painfully aware that a pair of murders had been committed on their doorstep within a few days of each other. Every dawn that broke without another corpse seemed to add to the tension instead of alleviating it. Police swarmed through the flop-houses of every major town. Showing up randomly at the doors of anyone with a room to rent to check that nothing untoward was happening. All eyes were open and the whole nation had its attention turned towards California.

Earle struck in Washington State. Florence Monks's strangled corpse was discovered behind the basement furnace of her home in Seattle. Yet once more, the police did not immediately make the connection to the Dark Strangler. Everyone still believed that he was in California. It was almost ridiculous to think that he might have leapt north by two states in so short a time. People may have spoken about him like he was some supernatural force, but he couldn't teleport. Besides, there were signs of a robbery in the Monk household. Her diamond ring had been stripped from her finger. Money had been taken from her purse. Other items of jewellery had vanished, too. If the police had the choice of believing that the corpse-stuffing was just a coincidence, then they were going to latch onto that possibility with both hands. In total, more than ten thousand dollars' worth of goods were taken from the Monk home. None of the previous garish news reports about the Gorilla Killer murders had included the detail that he robbed his victims. Poor reporting, focused solely on the prurient aspects of the case, had skipped over the details that might have helped connect the dots. Combined with the lack of information shared between police departments, this meant that Earle slipped through the cracks once more.

Adrian Harris arrived at the Portland rooming house of Edna Gaylord at ten in the morning on November 25. He was shabbily dressed in dark colours, but quietly charming towards both Edna herself and her regular tenant, Sophie Yates. He paid for a week in advance, dropped off his case, then settled in to chat with the women in the house's reception room. As always, Edna was complaining of her dire financial situation to all who'd listen, claiming that she didn't even have the money for a Thanksgiving Dinner this year. Adrian rose abruptly in the middle of her litany of complaints and left the building. Sophie found this hilarious. Edna, not so much. Yet just a short time later, Adrian returned with a roast and all the trimmings, ready to cook. Now they could all have Thanksgiving Dinner together. Just him and the two women, one just a little older than him, one the matriarch. The ever-repeating pattern of women in his life.

They dined together that night, drinking and eating well, Adrian quiet but contented as he listened to Edna and Sophie's quips back and forth. Sophie felt his burning eyes on her many times and suspected that he might come knocking on her door in the dark of the night, but Adrian was not so forward as that. It seemed that he meant to make their flirtation last out the whole week of his rental, though Sophie wasn't even sure that he realised that she was flirting with him half the time. Men could be so oblivious.

Adrian was not oblivious - he simply had no interest in the affections of a woman who was still breathing. Adrian may have strolled out of the boarding house with a smile on his face on the morning of the 29th, but it was Earle who stalked the streets in his clothing.

Blanche Myers was a longstanding boarding house operator of Portland, well-known among those who travelled to and from the city. While only in her 40s, she had earned a small fortune for herself through managing a variety of small businesses and rentals. She had no fear of the Gorilla Killer. It was widely known that he was still down in California, so she didn't think twice about showing the Mr Williams who enquired about a room to let into her home.

Earle strangled her to death with a handkerchief and a smile on his face. He carried her corpse up to her bedroom and raped her remains on her bed. When he was done with his pleasure, he stuffed her under the iron bedframe like an old blanket. With that done, he left bloody fingerprints on a bed knob, pulling himself to his feet, and headed out.

While he still had two days paid up, Adrian set to packing up the moment he returned to the boarding house, much to the dismay of the two women who'd been enjoying his company and his generosity up until this point. Digging through his bags, he presented Edna and Sophie with a piece of jewellery each as an early Christmas gift, and in thanks for their company. It was beyond a generous gift. The necklace and the ring that he had offered them were worth almost as much as the boarding house itself.

After Adrian departed, news spread of the murder, and so, too, did leaked information from the police that some items of clothing had been pawned in Portland that had belonged to a Mrs Florence Monk from up in Seattle. Items that had been stolen by the man that was now believed to be the Gorilla Killer.

Before even a day had passed, Edna and Sophie approached the police with their gifts and had their suspicions confirmed. Both were from Monk's home. The Dark Strangler had bought them dinner, slept under their roof, and fooled them entirely with his mask of sanity until a murder in their own back yard forced them to acknowledge who he was.

The whole West Coast went berserk. A killer was among them, and nothing was being done to stop his campaign of terror. The police and politicians came under immense pressure to deliver Earle up as a sacrificial lamb to win back the public trust, yet they could not provide him. Once more, he had slipped between their fingers. His legend continued to grow.

December stretched on with dull dread paving the streets of California thicker than any snow ever would. Still, Earle remained invisible.

Two thousand miles away from the horrors that Earle had left in his wake, Almira Brerard was coming home for Christmas. She had spent much of the last year in a psychiatric ward following a mental breakdown as a direct result of the degeneration of her marriage. Yet she had been showing steady improvement to her mental state throughout her hospitalisation, now managing to plaster a fake smile on her face whenever she was observed. It was sufficient for the staff to discharge her. At 41, she was already an old maid by the standards of the day, doomed to a lifetime alone in the wake of her inability to maintain her first marriage. Yet still, she managed to smile and steel herself against that reality as the doctors demanded. If it meant she could be free, she would tell any lie that they wanted to hear.

The family home in Council Bluffs, Iowa, had been ceded to her in the divorce, but she now found the place far too large and empty for her needs. There were too many rooms with too few bodies. The silence here was almost worse than the screams that haunted every night in the hospital. She sought a boarder in the local paper. She had no fear of any Dark

Strangler. The whole time that Earle's campaign of terror had been waged, she had been sequestered away with no access to the news, particularly any news that might be found distressing to a lady of delicate temperament. Even if she had been reading the papers religiously, there was no connection between the killings half a continent away and her own spare room.

When Mr Williams arrived on her doorstep, he seemed to be everything that she had hoped for in a boarder. Even her nosy neighbour peeking over the top of the fence seemed to approve, and they approved of literally nothing that Almira did. Williams was a quiet, unassuming man of about thirty years, polite to a fault and delicate in his discussions of her unusual living situation. He remained the perfect tenant right up until the moment that he looped a silk cord around her neck while her back was turned and bore her down to the ground. She died so quickly, there was no sign of a struggle when Earle was done. He carried her carefully to the bedroom before having his violent way with her remains. In her forties, she was a poor fit for either the grandmother that he liked to desecrate or the younger girls that revived his teenaged lusts. It seemed like he was at a loss what to do with her as a result. In the end, he settled for smoothing out her clothes and departing.

Just as Portland had not believed that the Gorilla Killer could strike at them so soon after his crimes in California, so too were the Iowa police in denial once Brerard's body was discovered. This far from the West Coast, the possibility didn't even enter their minds. This wasn't the Wild West - Iowa was a settled place where normal people lived their normal lives. What had started as a murder investigation was quickly translated into the discovery of a suicide. After all, the woman was barely out of a mental ward. Of course she had taken her own life.

The only fly in that ointment was the rape. There was plenty of physical evidence that Almira had been molested after her death, and the evidence implying that she had taken her own life was weak, at best. Reluctantly, the police re-opened their investigation into her death, but still no connection was made to the Dark Strangler case.

Christmas came and went, distracting both the public and the police from the investigation.

Earle was not so easily distracted from his goals. On December 27, he murdered and raped Bonnie Pace, a 23-year-old woman in Kansas City, Missouri. There was a room-to-let sign posted in the window of the house that she managed with her husband, and her corpse was shoved under her marital bed after he was done with her. This seemed to be his new favourite hiding place.

Germania Harpin suffered the same fate the very next day, every detail of the slaughter playing out in just the same way. He strangled her with a rag, he dragged her to bed, he raped her corpse, he shoved it under the bed. Earle was on the way out of the house when an unfamiliar sound gave him pause.

A baby was crying. It had been far too long since his childhood for Earle to remember being in that same situation, screaming and screaming as the baby of a dead mother. Yet still, the sound distracted him from his usual hasty getaway. He stopped in the hall and went back up the stairs to the nursery where little baby Robert, only eight months old, lay swaddled in his crib. He had been down for a nap when Germania went to show the room, but more than an hour had passed since then, and now Robert was crying out for her. He was hungry. He was alone. He was afraid.

Hands as big as his whole body reached down into his crib, tugging the swaddling blankets away and leaving him bare to the cold air. He did not know the man looming over him. He did not know these huge, strange hands. He screamed and he screamed as Earle removed the baby's cloth diaper, twisted it into a garotte and looped it around Robert's tiny pink neck. Just a tug would have been sufficient to end it all, but instead, Earle tightened the terrycloth slowly, cutting off the screams, then the baby's breath.

To any other man, this might have represented the ultimate departure from morality. For Earle, it barely raised an eyebrow. His own nightmare life, viewed through a lens darkly, justified strangling babes in their cradles. He was sparing the child the suffering of life. Every woman that he met could be moulded to situate one of the archetypes that he had encountered, but men had no place in the Gospel of Earl. He was the only man in the shadowed world where he dwelled, so any man or boy that he met must simply have been him at some other stage in his life.

When he had met other grown men, he assumed that they were monsters inside. When brothers spoke to their sisters, he assumed that there was lust simmering beneath the surface. When he came upon a baby, stripped of its mother before it could even form an impression of the world, the best that he could imagine for it was death before it could be corrupted. His self-loathing ran so deep that even now he could not think of any fate better than death.

Nineteen twenty-six ended on that note, with the suddenly sombre press faced with reporting not just another gruesome

Gorilla Killer attack, but brutal infanticide. Many national papers refused to run the story. Other censored it heavily. Regardless, what had until now been viewed by much of the public as a fun little horror story had taken a turn into darkness too deep to be comprehended.

With You I Break Nations

The Dark Strangler could be anywhere. He could lunge out of any shadow. He could be knocking at your door right now. The United States of America was in a state of abject panic. Women were afraid to walk the streets alone even in the safest of neighbourhoods. There was no end in sight.

For three months, the police pursued every lead to a dead end. For three months, the families of the victims spoke out, demanding, and then finally begging for justice to be done. It was as though the world was speaking to the Strangler himself to come forward, to act again, to be seen. Time was not enough to make people forget him now. The invisibility that he had enjoyed must surely falter in the face of the whole country hunting for him.

On April 27, Earle strangled Mary McConnell to death, raped her body, and robbed her Philadelphia, Pennsylvania, townhouse. He worked methodically through the home once he was done with the things that his nature compelled him to do, collecting anything of value, with the intention of pawning it and earning himself a pretty penny. He was numb to the reality of what he was now – he accepted himself fully, hating the sin but loving the sinner – so that meant it was time to take off the hair-shirt that he had been wearing and start living in some comfort between his killings. His rational mind was allowed a seat at the decision-making table. It was ragged and ruined after so long pushed to the periphery, and he was unlikely to be winning any battles of wits in the near future, but something resembling rationality came back into his actions, a fusion of his compulsions and his criminal experience finally brought to bear. Observing the ever-tightening dragnet to the west, he headed further east, still maintaining a low profile for now.

In May, Earle arrived in Buffalo, New York, where he intended to lie low until the nationwide manhunt began to cool down a little. Normally he moved on as much out of necessity as to avoid capture, but with the takings from the McConnell home, he had enough to set himself up for a good stretch. Everything would have worked out fine if the local pawn shop owner hadn't been such a stickler for the rules. He refused to buy the clearly stolen goods that Earle brought in, and he went a step further by carefully documenting each of the items before informing Earle of this fact.

Earle returned to his boarding house still as destitute as when he had arrived but filled with a fresh wave of rage. When he had allowed fate to guide him fully and given himself over to God's will, he had not suffered a single setback, yet now that he was trying to do the bare minimum required to maintain his own living standard, he was somehow thwarted at every turn.

He took it as a sign that he was not meant to remain in New York State, a sign that the Lord wanted him to move on with all alacrity. For a moment, he tried to ascribe it to the mysterious ways of the Lord, but then he recalled that he was not like other men. If the Lord meant for him to move on from New York, it must be because there was a message to be left here.

Jennie Randolph had suffered the worst thing to afflict any parent - she had lost her son. Drowning in her grief, she had taken to doing charity work for the YMCA in Buffalo to help keep her mind off the terrible event. With her husband already shuffled off the mortal coil, it fell to her brother Gideon Gillette to keep her company during her recovery. He had moved into her house with her and, as a practical man, he had been pressing her to start renting out her boy's old room to a boarder. To fill up the house with life again instead of wallowing in old memories.

Jennie was resistant to the idea but so worn down by this point that she'd accept just about anything if it meant she didn't have to think about it too hard. She allowed Gideon to put a listing in the local paper for the room to rent, hoping that it would go unanswered and that this would be the end of it.

She was upstairs when she heard the knock on the front door that day, lying in the dark of her curtained room, staring up at the ceiling and pretending that she didn't exist. It wasn't going to be her boy at the door, so why should she care that there was somebody there? Why were people always coming here to bother her – even her brother, bless him, had been more of a nuisance than a help. She had spent her life caring for other people, and now that those people were all gone, she felt like she had earned some respite, but instead here came the whole world knocking at her door, demanding her attention, as though she had it to spare. Maybe if she just lay here in the dark until she melted away, the world would stop pressing in and she could be left at peace with her sorrow. Maybe if she stayed silent, people who knew nothing of suffering would stop popping up to hammer her with platitudes. There was a sound of movement downstairs. Gideon was in. He'd been waiting for her to answer the door, and now she could hear the petulant stomp to his feet as he went to do it himself. He hadn't changed since he was a toddler. She'd lived her whole life, loved and lost, and he still stomped his feet when he had to answer the door. It didn't seem right.

There was a muffled conversation at the door, then Gideon called out her name. He couldn't even answer the door without dragging her into it. What had she done to be cursed with this kindly helper in her time of grief? If he'd just leave her alone, she could feel things and move past them, but instead, she had to pretend every day that she was fine. She had to crush all her misery down. He called again. With a groan, Jennie pulled herself up out of bed, straightened out her silhouette in the dark mirror, and headed down.

Gideon was his usual excitable self when she came down. The wisps of white hair on top of his head swaying around as he introduced her to Charles Harrison, a painter from New York, who was interested in renting out their room. Harrison was hulking and sombrely dressed, yet his politeness and even quietness compared to the racket that Gideon made was a balm to any fears that Jennie might have experienced. His face lit up, ever so briefly, when he caught sight of her, like he had been waiting a long time to meet her and she was living up to every expectation.

They discussed terms and showed him the room, and after he left, Jennie still didn't know if he wanted to take the place or not. He wanted to sleep on it, supposedly, and while at the start of the conversation, she would have been quite happy for the man to walk off into the sea if it meant he wouldn't be troubling her any more, now she found that there was a twinge of regret in her heart. She wanted Mr Harrison to stay. He was a mite younger than her son had been, but the quiet way that he deferred to her in all things reminded her so much of the boy that had been that it drew out a fresh flood of tears as soon as she got herself some time alone. Loath as she was to admit it, Gideon was right - this new lodger might be just the thing to bring her suffering to an end.

By the time that the darkly dressed stranger had stormed out of his pawn shop, the owner was already compiling his report to the police to see if the offerings matched up to any known burglaries about town.

The local police could not make the connection themselves, but they were convinced enough by the pawnbroker's description of events to spread the itemised list a little further afield. First, it was wired to the major cities nearby, then the major cities in other states, then finally it began to propagate out to the smaller towns, where it was perfectly matched with the list of items stolen from Mary McConnell.

Yet even when this news came back to the local police three days later on the thirtieth, they were too distracted to care. There had been a gruesome murder in Buffalo, the kind that they had never expected to see outside of the big city. A kindly local woman had been strangled to death and raped in her own home in the middle of the day. Her brother had come home to discover her remains crammed under an unmade bed, blood leaking out onto the carpet.

It had all the hallmarks of a killing by the Dark Strangler, and when presented with that killer's description, Gideon immediately burst into tears. Charles Harrison was the Gorilla Killer, and he had invited him into his sister's home. He had made the arrangements, posted the advert. This was all his fault. Pushing his sister into things that she didn't want to do to ease his guilt and the financial burden of supporting her.

He had doomed his sister to a fate worse than death by his actions, and he could not live with that burden. Guilt more than grief drove him to draw out his old army service revolver and place it against his temple. Before any sort of justice could be brought to bear against Earle Nelson, Gideon had taken his own life.

Slipping past the police dragnet once more, Earle sought out another new city and another fresh set of victims who were not expecting him. In Detroit, he found exactly that. Earle did not pause or falter. He did not slow or hesitate. He walked straight from the trainyard to the house of his next victims, and he walked through the steps of his pattern with a precision that boggles the mind.

Fanny May was sixty years old. Her boarding house had been operating for over a decade, and she had many residents who had lived with her for the full length of that time, thanks to her good nature. It was rare for her to have a spare room open up, and she was selective about the people that she offered them to. So it was that Earle had to interview with her, and longstanding resident Maureen Oswald-Athory, to decide if he would be a good fit for the culture of the place. The two women sat there in judgement of him, one an old matronly type, the other younger, looking like she might be the old woman's daughter. They were looking him up and down, trying to decide if he was sufficiently civilised, trying to decide if he was worthy of living under their roof. It touched some dark part of his brain.

Maureen was tasked with showing him the room as Fanny May didn't much like to hike up and down the stairs if she didn't need to. The two of them went upstairs and silence fell over the house. Time stretched on, but Fanny May still didn't stir from her seat, concocting excuses for the pair so that she didn't have to get up. She might have gone on sitting there for an hour if the lights hadn't died. She was a polite woman, but there was nobody around to hear her, so she cursed. Candles never blew a fuse. Electricity was new and exciting, but it was also a damned nuisance when it did things like this.

Well, there wasn't a chance in hell she was going down the stairs to look for the fuse box, so she went up instead, using the light still filtering in through the windows as her guide. At the top of the stairs, a rhythmic thumping caught her attention, and with a frown, she headed along to the spare room. Inside, the new lodger was raping Maureen. The lamp on the bedside table was knocked askew, the electrical cord cut clean off and looped around the dead woman's throat so tight that Fanny could see blood oozing out around it. She must have made some involuntary sound, a gasp or a retch because the new lodger's head snapped around and his dark eyes bore into her.

She didn't even cry out. She was so mesmerised by the sight of him rising up from the corpse and strolling across the room as though it were the most natural thing in the world. Her eyes flicked down to the obscenity jutting up from between his legs, aimed at her like a gun. The scene took her so thoroughly by surprise that the man was upon her, closing his hands on her throat before she even thought to run.

Earle killed them both, raped them both, ransacked the house, and took everything of value. He sold off as much of his newly acquired goods in the local pawn shops as he could, breaking his ill-gained goods up into bundles of similar materials and trying different places so that the full picture of his burglaries couldn't be composed. It was a smart move for a man of such questionable intelligence. While he may have lacked in some areas, he made up for it in criminal acuity.

The police were called when a neighbour realised that the lights in the house had been on for several days, and the bodies were discovered. In the chaos that Earle had wrought on the place, it didn't even cross the mind of the police that this could be the work of the strangler until it was too late.

The day after the slaughter and chaos in Detroit, Earle arrived in Chicago, Illinois, with his lusts and fury replenished by a long night rolling around a freight car's empty belly. He didn't even bother to find a place to sleep that night before heading to the home and boarding rooms of Mary Sietsma. Just as with every other victim, he charmed his way inside using the Bible as a talisman of his goodwill and high moral values. Just as with every other victim, he gave no warning before pouncing on the poor woman and hauling her to the corner of the bedroom he'd supposedly had an interest in renting from her. This time he didn't even bother to cut the electrical cord off the lamp before he used it as a garotte, throttling the life out of Mary. It wasn't like there was much life left to choke out of her after he had smashed her head into the ground a couple of times, shattering her skull.

This time he did not steal everything that was not nailed down. He had to travel light from here on out. While he had been allowing his base instincts and the Lord above to guide him through those past few days, his rational mind was freed up to concentrate on the larger problem of avoiding detection and arrest.

His solution was elegant in its simplicity. There was nowhere left in the United States that he could hope to go where his reputation did not precede him. For every one appointment he had been able to make and transform into a satisfactory murder, there had been dozens of women who were properly guarding themselves against him, ensuring that they were never alone with a strange man, and all because of the spectre of the Gorilla Killer hanging over them. There was only one option that Earle could see to escape all of this. He was going to have to leave America for the first time in his life and seek out pastures new.

They Will Pass Like Wild Flowers

Winnipeg sat across the border in Canada, the largest city that Earle had heard of in the Great White North. There was no border to cross for a hobo, and the lines drawn on maps meant nothing to the Lord in Heaven. A simple train ride took Earle out of the reach of American authorities. With no further commandments immediately revealing themselves from on high, Earle was free to pursue the course that he felt was the most logical. In a thrift shop, he traded his fancy suit for a workman's outfit and a dollar, completely changing his appearance from what had been reported in every paper in an instant. He was a stranger in a strange land, so there was no reason to continue holding himself to his grandmother's standards of dress. It wasn't like there was any more shame that he could bring her.

With the plain clothes of a workman, he would fit in anywhere. The rich would think he was there to do some menial task, the poor would see him as one of their own to be shielded from the eyes of the law. It was the perfect disguise. It would cost him some points when he meant to charm his way into places, of course, but he had no intention of killing anyone anytime soon. He needed some respite. The Lord had sent so many willing bodies to his hands over the past few weeks that even his lusts could not keep up. It had been only six days since his last kill. For now, at least, he could pretend that he was just a normal man going about his normal business.

Mr Woodcots was a charming man for someone of such obviously low birth. Usually, Catherine Hill's house at 133 Smith Street in Winnipeg was reserved only for gentlemen of better stature, yet she couldn't help but feel that there would be some value to having such a man living under her roof. There were always odd jobs needing tending, and if she could offer a discount to Woodcot's rate in exchange for him conducting repairs for her, then it was a good deal for the both of them. He paid for a week up front, which was both a surprise and a relief to Catherine, then settled into the attic room that she had set aside for him without complaint. The last that she saw of him that first day, he was sitting on his bed, Bible clasped in hand and eyes closed, just listening to the quiet of the neighbourhood outside. For someone with the look of a brute, she wondered if he might not have the soul of a poet buried somewhere beneath the surface. His head swayed from side to side, almost imperceptibly, as though he was listening to music that nobody else could hear. She left him with a smile on her face. He would be a good fit for the house.

As he once had in San Francisco, Earle now walked the streets of Winnipeg invisibly, observing but not interacting, closer than ever to his reputation as some sort of spectre. He drifted through the quiet suburban neighbourhood where he had planted himself like a feather on the wind - until he saw her.

Lola Cowans was actually one of his neighbours on Smith Street, though there was no way he could have known that on first spotting her. At fourteen years old, she was the very image of innocence downtrodden. If Aunt Lillian had been damned to a life of poverty before he first met her, Lola Cowans would have been what she looked like on the first day that they met. While Lillian had tormented him when she was a teenager, both deliberately with her words and actions, and accidentally with her budding body, this version would have done no such thing. This version would have known suffering and exhaustion and been just like him. Another animal from the gutters, one who was willing to run wild with him, willing to get dirty, willing to rut with him, willing to be everything that he had always wanted his Lillian to be.

The course of his day changed. He trailed after her at a distance, never approaching, but always watching.

Lola's family had fallen on hard times. Her mother had died a few years back, and her father was now laid up in bed with a case of pneumonia that would later prove to be fatal. They had a roof over their heads but no means of paying the next month's rent with Mr Cowans incapable of getting out of bed. Her little brother had some skill with his hands, so he folded paper into pretty little flowers, and Lola took them out to sell in the streets, travelling door to door and hoping desperately for some kindness from strangers. So far, they had earned enough to feed the family every few days, but without more money soon, there was no hope that Lola's father might recover. Disease was eating away at him from the inside, shrinking him smaller and smaller with every passing day.

It took Earle all day to approach her, and we will never know what offer he made that made her follow him back to his boarding house room. It was clear that money was involved, but no small amount of charm must have entered the equation, too. Lola was nobody's fool. She had encountered the worst that Winnipeg had to offer in terms of the grasping hands of older men, so it would have taken quite an offer to bring her into the bedroom of a strange man. Earle did not lack money, nor did he lack the gentle giant act that might have set even Lola's nerves to rest.

Once he had the little girl alone, he wrapped a length of rope around her throat and strangled her until she was on the verge of death. Not dead, but on its doorstep. She was too precious to him for him to allow this to end so soon. He needed every part of this act of divine love to last as long as it could. Still on the border between life and death, between awareness and blissful darkness, Lola watched him stripping off her clothes and then his own. She watched as his shaking, reverent hands traced over the harsh lines of her starved physique. She could not feel all of the things that he did to her. The rope at her throat ensured a precious numbness that prevented most of the horror from reaching her. Yet she was still aware enough, during his mounting of her, that tears flowed freely down her face. She tried to fight him, she tried to stop him. Even half-dead and damaged beyond all repair by the noose at her throat, she dug her nails into his arms, scratched at his scalp, fought him feebly.

Earle did not appreciate this intrusion on his pleasure. He brought her fingers to his lips, and bit down, hooking under her fingernails and then levering them up until they snapped off in a pop of blood. Ten times he repeated this mutilation, all while still raping the poor girl.

When she tried to slap at him, he took hold of her hand and snapped the wrist joint. When she managed to squeeze her legs together tightly enough to slow his implacable thrusts, he snapped her thigh bones like another man would have broken a stick for the fire.

No other victim ever suffered like Lola Cowan. For the dreadful sin of reminding him of both the women he wanted and the world he had come from, she was allowed to live and suffer through the degradations he usually reserved for the dead.

Bleeding, broken, ruined, Lola must have been longing for death long before it came, yet even when it seemed that Earle was done with her, he did not tighten the rope any further. She could not speak, she could not draw a real breath, but still she lived when he picked her up and pushed her into the space beneath the bed.

She lay down there in the dark, bleeding from every one of the awful injuries that Earle had inflicted, too bruised and broken to even move. She lay there and listened as he knelt by the side of the bed, said his prayers and then climbed on top of her once more. Separated this time by the thin mattress and springs of the cot, his weight still pressed down on her, crushing that last little bit of life out of her body as he began to snore.

Come morning, he hauled her dead body out from under the bed and raped her all over again. After all the damage he had already wrought to her skinny frame, there wasn't much left of her when he shoved her back under the bed once more.

There were more broken bones in her body than whole ones, blood leaking from every orifice.

Catherine Hill came up the stairs to do her regular daily tidy up and discovered that Mr Woodcot's door was ajar. Knocking, she pushed it open to find that both the man and his battered old suitcase had disappeared. It was quite bizarre. Why he would abandon his room with days still paid up? With a sigh at all of the possibilities that she'd just missed out on, she went in and gave the place a spruce up. It barely needed cleaning. Woodcot had taken good care of the place, made little mess, even made his bed before departing. If anything, it was probably cleaner than when he first arrived. She could swear the man had dusted.

She need not have worried about missing out on any money either. If anything, she was making more, with Woodcot's cash already in her pocket and a new lodger moving in the next day.

Lola's family searched for her fruitlessly, but with only a pre-teen available to do any searching or make any enquiries, it should not have been a surprise that the girl was not found or the authorities even made aware that she was missing.

Earle had not expected so precious a gift to be presented to him by God, and now that he had departed and knew that the time he had left in the city was running short, he found himself compelled to complete the murder of the only other woman that existed in his world. The crone to match the maiden he had just massacred.

He rode the street car across town, chatting away amicably with the other passengers and even giving a bare-headed man his hat to thank him for the fine conversation. He visited second-hand stores, contemplating purchases and flashing a roll of bills that caught the attention of many a shopkeeper.

Eventually, across town, he caught a glimpse of Emily Patterson as she set about cleaning her home. Something about the image of that woman framed in the bay windows captivated him. She was not old enough to be his grandmother, not really, but there was something about her manner that he found so motherly, he had no choice but to pursue her. The 'room to let' sign in the corner of that window was all that it took to give him certainty. God wanted this or he would not have given the sign.

He brought all of his charm to bear on her, stating up front that he had no money but would be more than willing to help out around the house in exchange for the first week's rent. Emily wasn't sure at first. She was intrigued by this odd man but unclear on his intentions. At his request, she brought out her husband's toolbox for him to use, and he set about repairing the faulty hinge on the screen door. Neighbours passed and he greeted them with a nod as he saw to his work. He had always been good with his hands; this task was easily within his capabilities. When all was said and done, Emily could not deny that the work had been done well. She asked him to bring the tools back inside and agreed to talk about the possibility of letting him the room.

When he came in, there was a bashful smile on his face, and Emily couldn't help but return it. For all that he was a grown man, he had the charm of a young boy. He thanked her profusely as he crossed the hall, voice getting softer and softer as he approached. His thanks and blessings were only a hoarse whisper when he was in arm's reach.

He hefted the hammer he had been using only a moment before to help her and brought it down hard on the top of her head. Emily fell like a puppet with cut strings, toppling to a heap on the floor. Not dead, not unconscious, but rendered immobile by the first blow. He brought the hammer down on her again. Then again.

If he had not pressed his face beside hers as he tightened the twisted rag from his belt around her throat, she never would have heard his endless litany of thanks as he choked the life out of her. Twisting and pulling and blessing her with every breath until she was gone.

Catherine Hill's new lodger was full of complaints. The bed was uncomfortable. There was a foul smell in the room. The sun came in through the skylight too early in the day and woke him before he was ready. If only Mr Woodcot was still here. That man had been a class act by comparison. Grumbling all the way up the stairs, Catherine made her way to the attic room, mainly to prove to herself that all these complaints were unwarranted.

The smell hit her in the hall. Giving her pause. It really did stink up here. Maybe a rat had died under the floorboards again. That was always a hellish problem to fix, levering up boards and peering around by lamplight. If only Mr Woodcot was still here, she could have delegated the job to him. When she opened the door to the room, there was a cloud of flies lingering and the stench made her gag.

There was something seriously rotten in the room, and the new man was right enough that it seemed to be emanating from the bed. Crouching down, she lifted up the bedframe's valance to check what had been left behind to create such a stench. The other tenants found her fainted dead away, and even when Catherine managed to get her thoughts in enough order to recount what she had seen, they didn't believe it until they saw it with their own eyes. The police came, saw, and rushed off to make rapid use of the house's communal restroom. The thing under the bed could barely be recognised as human anymore. The angles of the limbs were wrong. The shapes had been crushed out of their usual forms. It would fall to the medical examiner to prove that the body was intact and no part of it was missing by a process not unlike assembling a jigsaw. Rot had not made that puzzle easier to solve.

Mr Patterson had returned home from work to find no trace of his wife. He was concerned, to say the least, and before the day was out, he reported her absence to the police. He and his neighbours searched the house from top to bottom for any sign of her, but she was not to be found. With two children in the house, Emily's husband had no choice but to press on with the usual routine, feeding them, bathing them and tucking them into bed to the best of his ability, doing what he could to calm their anxieties while his dread fought to overcome him. He had no doubt in his mind that something terrible had happened to his wife. He had no doubt that she was dead. He knelt by his son's bedside and prayed to the Lord above to show him where his wife had gone. For long moments, he stayed knelt there, desperate for the knowledge, but when it seemed that no word from on high was coming, he stood up, knee catching on the valance skirt around the bottom of his son's bed, lifting it up and revealing the gory mess that had been stuffed beneath.

When the police arrived, their search of the house was considerably more meticulous than Mr Patterson and his neighbours had accomplished. A brown whipcord suit was found to be missing, along with seventy dollars in cash that the family had put away for a rainy day. More telling than what had been taken was what had been left behind. Earle's workman's garb had been stuffed under the bed with the naked body of Emily. He had walked out wearing the new suit. Tangled up in the clothes that he'd left behind was a little knife. Barely even large enough to be considered a weapon really, more of a tool that handymen might keep around. The blade was blackened at one point where it had been used to cut through a live electrical wire. This tiny piece of forensic evidence tied this horrific murder to the butchery that had been going on in America over the past year through the cases of Athory and May. The Dark Strangler was in Canada, and this knife proved it more surely than any amount of similarities between crime scenes.

The Chief of Detectives for Winnipeg, George Smith, picked up the case himself, going back to the basics of investigation and reconstructing every step that their killer had taken from the door of the Patterson house onwards. All information that could be scoured from witnesses was acquired, every inch of the room where Lola Cowan was found was searched, everyone who had seen her on the day of her disappearance was interviewed. Just as Earle moved forward relentlessly, so too did George Smith. But while the Dark Strangler had only himself and his wits to rely on, Smith had the full weight of authority and manpower that had been vested in him to conduct his pursuit.

The brown whipcord suit had been sold at Sam Waldman's Second Hand Store at 629 Main Street, a mere hour after the proposed time of death of Mrs Patterson. He had traded it for a plain black suit that was actually his size. Every detail of it was copied out from Waldman's receipts and memory.

Next door in the Central Barber Shop, Earle went in for his customary shave, haircut, and massage. The owner, Nick Tabor, noticed dried blood and scabs on Earle's scalp as he worked, and when he commented on them, Earle's entire demeanour shifted, and he growled at the man to mind his business and not to touch them. Tabor was an amateur phrenologist, so he was able to note down every detail of Earle's appearance, right down to the size of his skull, when the police came by to take his evidence.

Witness by witness. Step by step. The police tracked Earle. The streetcar operator saw him boarding on Portage Avenue and disembarking at Headingley.

Hugh Elder shared a car with Earle to Portage La Prairie, with the broad man offering up the majority of the fare in exchange for a rapid departure. It was there that the trail went cold. It was still the same day as Earle's departure, so anyone who operated a car running out of town would have been bedding down at their destination before returning the following day. There were cars departing from Portage La Prairie heading out to Brandon, Regina, Saskatoon, and Calgary. Any one of which might have carried the Dark Strangler away to safety.

If it had been a simple foot pursuit, then Earle would have thwarted George Smith at that moment, but once again, the detective had resources at his disposal that would not have even crossed the murderer's mind. Telegrams and phone calls went out to every newspaper in every town that Earle might feasibly have reached. His name, his aliases, his description, every detail of every item of clothing that he was wearing, every detail of every stolen object that he was carrying, they were delivered not only to every police department across Canada but to every newspaper, too, pasted across their front covers along with every photograph that had ever been taken of the man. Most crushingly of all, Smith made a quick whip around of the upper classes and came back with the promise of a $1500 reward for information that led to the Dark Strangler's apprehension.

Earle had survived through all of his years because of his invisibility. In one fell stroke, Smith had robbed him of it.

I Will Send for Many Hunters

In Regina, Saskatchewan, a Mr Harry Harcout was renting a room for one night in Mary Rowe's boarding house. He woke early on Monday the 13th of June before the rest of the house had even stirred in their beds, and he went down to read the paper.

He flew back up the stairs in a rage, ripping the clothes off his back, discarding almost every item of clothing in his case by tossing it onto the trash heap out back of the house. Every item of clothing that the paper described him as wearing, he abandoned. Wearing only the bare minimum to maintain decorum, he packed up the remainder of his belongings and headed into town. He entered the department store as they opened their doors for the day and was out again almost as fast with a new set of blue overalls, a shirt and a cap. From there he went straight to the Royal Second Hand Store to sell off the remainder of his clothing. It did not match the description of his known appearance from the paper that he had read, so he assumed that the store owner would make no connection. The clerk, noticing all the Winnipeg labels on the clothing, contacted the Regina police the moment that Earle was out of sight, and the hunt was hot on his heels again.

Instinct or divine intervention drove Earle to leave town immediately, and luck put him in the path of Isidore Silverman. Silverman was a scrap metal merchant who drove back and forth across the countryside, collecting what he could from the little farms and homes scattered between here and Manitoba. It would be a long meandering journey, but Earle insisted that he was in no hurry and would be happy enough to pay his way. Not willing to look a gift horse in the mouth and looking forward to the prospect of a little conversation during his long drive, Isidore shook his hand and hoisted him up into the van's cabin.

As Silverman travelled the back roads, visiting here and there, the main roads were awash with patrolling police cars. Detectives from across Canada were rushing to the last sighting of the Strangler in Regina and spreading out in organised search patterns from there, certain he must have been heading towards the American border.

The thought had certainly crossed Earle's mind. He had expected a fresh start-up in Canada, but instead, he'd encountered an organised and focused police department that was more interested in stopping his crimes than acquiring the personal glory of cuffing him themselves. After days on the road with Silverman, Earle arrived at Boissevain, Manitoba. Even this smaller town was crawling with the police, so he didn't pause for a moment. No sooner was he out of

Silverman's truck than he was back on the road with a thumb held up, looking to hitch a ride.

Despite all the ruckus in town, the people living around Boissevain didn't truly believe that anything bad could be going on in their neighbourhood. When they saw a down-on-his-luck man hitchhiking at the side of the road, their natural kindness won out. Earle was polite and pleasant to the farmer who picked him up, but not particularly chatty because the long-silent thinking parts of his mind were buzzing with activity, trying to work out how he was being followed, trying to work out how to avoid detection and get back to the United States where no such concerted effort had ever been made to capture him. Each time that one of his rides made it to another tiny bastion of civilisation in the middle of rural Canada, he hopped right out, thanking them profusely, waited until they'd moved on over the horizon and started hitching all over again. He had worked out that his movements were being traced through witnesses, so he was doing the only thing that he could to provide a tangle of loose threads for the police to untangle. Every time he caught a new ride and got off in a new town, there was another step that the police might miss, setting him free of their scrutiny. He took a half dozen separate rides through that first day, making it to Wakopa, just five miles from the U.S. border. There was no possibility his pursuers were still on his tail. He was certain that he had shaken them.

Proud as punch, he strolled into Morgan's General Store on Wakopa's main street just a little after six in the afternoon. He bought himself a soda, some bread, and some cheese, then settled down on the porch outside the store to eat his dinner. Leslie Morgan, the owner of the store, stood opposite a rack of newspapers all day, every day. The face of the Gorilla Killer had been staring him in the face for days. He knew it like the back of his hand. The moment that Earle was out the door of the shop, he picked up the telephone and called the police.

Constable WA Gray was the only member of the Manitoba Provincial Police on duty, but he dropped everything and raced to Wakopa with all haste. The moments ticked away, with Earle happily devouring his meal and Gray driving so fast that he almost came off the road at every corner. The sheer size of the province, which had been to Earle's detriment all day as he tried to cross it and make his escape, was now protecting him just as surely as his anonymity had. Leslie Morgan was forced to stand and watch as the serial murderer finished up his dinner, brushed off the crumbs, and walked away.

Five miles was nothing to Earle. He was used to walking from dawn to dusk and beyond. Setting off at a leisurely pace, he was liable to reach the border in the dark of night. The perfect time to cross over undetected and return to an easy life of theft and slaughter.

Gray came to Wakopa and tumbled out his car with his pistol already drawn. He ran into the General Store only to see the sorrow on Leslie's face and the shake of his head. "Which way was he headed?"

On foot, heading cross country, Constable Gray chased after the serial murderer Earle Nelson. For hours, as the sun went down, he tracked him by footprints in the mud, broken branches, and rabbit-trails. Eventually, they crossed the train tracks, and there was a clear direction for both Earle and Gray to follow. The Constable hunted the hunter of women down like he was wild game and, finally, when he got the giant of a man in sight, he drew his service revolver and called out to him to stop.

Earle turned slowly to look at this interloper in the wilderness, this man whom he had never met, who for some reason had a gun drawn and aimed at him. He held up his hands, he made no sudden movements. He seemed to be perplexed more than anything else. In word and action, he gave no hint that he was a murderer. In fact, he insisted that he was Virgil Wilson, a day labourer and farm hand who was simply travelling in search of his next job. In all likelihood, this Virgil was a real man that Earle had met during his sojourns on the rails down in America. The truth had always been Earle's shield. He struggled to maintain any sort of lie for a length of time, tripping over his threads of deception, but if he had a true story that he could tell, he could recite it flawlessly as his Bible verses.

Regardless of the story that Earle was feeding him, Gray believed he had ample reason to hold him until his identity could be confirmed. The two men walked the two miles back along the tracks to Wakopa, then the constable cuffed the giant and placed him in the backseat of his car for the drive back to the jail at Killarney, Manitoba, the closest place with a cell to hold the man.

The jail cell on the side of the police station was barely large enough to contain the giant of a man. It was like a Medieval dungeon, a throwback to a hundred years before, when Europeans first settled in the region. A metal bedframe hung from the wall, topped off with a straw mattress. Methodically, Gray went through the motions of booking Earle in, having him remove his shoes, socks, and belt to prevent a suicide or escape attempt. With a sigh, 'Virgil' lay himself down on the bed and closed his eyes while Gray locked the door.

Once he was out of sight, he let his long-held breath escape him. He had never expected to encounter anything like this working as a deputy in the sticks. Secure in the knowledge that Earle wasn't going anywhere, he headed off to the general store to send a telegram to George Smith in Winnipeg, informing him of the capture and requesting assistance in confirming the identification. The physical description that Gray had received matched perfectly, but the intelligence gathered on Earle's clothing had not been updated since he had traded in the brown whipcord suit.

Taking a moment for himself, Gray bought a cigar and smoked it as he walked back to the police station. It wasn't every day that you caught one of the most notorious killers in the whole world - he deserved a little treat. Inside the police station, it was silent. The cell door hung open, the remains of a metal nail file still lodged inside its workings. Virgil had freed himself. The Dark Strangler was at large once more.

In a wild panic, Gray sprinted back to the General Store to send another telegraph, warning every police department in the surrounding area of what had happened.

Like a military general, George Smith sat with a map of Canada's provinces spread out before him, assigning his troops where he thought they might do the most good. When he had received the report of capture from Gray, he had not halted the search. There had been enough false captures and dead leads to keep his hopes thoroughly quashed. Yet when that second report came in, announcing this prisoner's escape, it changed his perception instantly. There was suddenly no doubt in his mind about the identity of this Virgil

Wilson. He deployed a whole train car of Winnipeg's finest to Manitoba, not to Killarney itself, but to the south of the border. He was planning ahead of the killer's moves instead of just chasing after him.

Throughout all of that day, Earle was lurking in the shadows at the periphery of Killarney, hiding amongst the long grain standing along the side of the railroad tracks. There was no way that he was going to make it on foot, but he still had his old perfect escape plan on standby. He climbed on top of the grain elevator just a little along from the station and lay in wait. When he heard the whistle blowing, he popped up for just a moment, like a prairie dog, to check the direction the train was headed. The train was southbound, heading for America. It was exactly what he needed.

It slowed right down as it was coming through town, for safety, and like so many times before, Earle let himself drop down off the grain tower to land on the top of the last train car as the locomotive was beginning to gain speed. He clambered down and let himself in through the door into what should have been the luggage car at the back. It was not. An additional car had been added to this train before it departed from Winnipeg to accommodate the full complement of policemen that had boarded. A cabin full of guns swung around to point at Earle, and for the second time in as many days, he had to hold up his hands and surrender.

There was no statute in place for arrests to be made in motion across provinces, so Earle had to take a seat and wait as they made the rest of the journey to Crystal City, where the whole troupe disembarked, placed him under arrest, and then climbed onto the next train back to Winnipeg, where justice awaited Earle.

His clothes were stripped from him and he was pushed into ill-fitting garb donated by one of the train's passengers. The clothes off his back were evidence, marking him as linked to the Winnipeg crimes. Every item that he was carrying was carefully detailed to George Smith's exacting standards. Now that they had their man, there was no possibility that he was going to slip through their fingers by destroying evidence or manipulating events after the fact.

From the train station to the police station on Rupert Street, there was a parade. The whole town, a crowd of over three thousand people, had turned out to see the Dark Strangler brought out into the light.

George Smith felt no need to meet the target of his great hunt face to face. They would only encounter one another months later in the courtroom when Smith provided his collected evidence to the jury.

Instead, Earle suffered through a parade of forty other visitors in the coming days. One witness after another came in to view the line-up of look-a-likes and Earle. Every single one of them looked into his hooded black eyes and declared him to be the killer.

Earle continued to deny everything, claiming that he was Virgil Wilson, claiming that all of the witnesses were either liars or fools. Even in the face of the landladies that he had not murdered, the witnesses who had seen him emerging from the scenes of his crimes. Even the people from his past were brought in - his aunt and uncle, his ex-wife, everyone who had ever known Earle Nelson came forth, pointed their finger and damned him. Even still, the Winnipeg court was not willing to press a case. Not until there was no shadow of a doubt about Earle's identity.

The captain of the San Francisco Police Department came to Canada himself with a copy of Earle Nelson's fingerprints in his case. As he stood by the prison cell, Earle's prints were taken again, and the two sheets were compared. It was a perfect match, the perfect evidence that Earle was exactly who they suspected he was. With a shrug, Virgil fell away from his shoulders and Earle was left behind in the cell, brows drawn down, gospel on his lips, a snarl in his voice.

He was indicted for the murder of Mrs Emily Patterson, for which the courts felt that they had the most incontrovertible evidence. They did not need to charge him for all of the crimes it was widely believed that he had committed. One trial and one hanging would be quite sufficient.

Detectives from across America came to visit Earle in his cell, practically begging him to accept responsibility for the crimes that he had committed so that their cases could be closed and the families of his victims could have their minds put at rest. He refused. Over and over he refused. Even though he was now willing to admit that he was Earle Nelson, he refused outright to accept any possibility that he had committed a crime. 'For a godly man like me, a crime such as murder is simply impossible.'

He quoted scripture relentlessly, as though the words of better men might save him from his reality. Even now, when the chase was done and death was certain, he still would not give up his façade of righteousness. Even in the dark of the night when nobody else was around, the guards could still hear him reciting Revelations to himself. He never seemed to sleep, he never seemed to stop. His religious mania was fuel for his body even when all else failed him. A source of comfort even to this devil given physical form.

Yet still more police came. There had been a trio of murders in San Francisco, just after Earle was released from Napa State Hospital, throughout the late summer of 1925.

Elizabeth Jones had been strangled with her own necklace after being seen speaking to a man interested in buying property from her. Daisy Anderson was found strangled and nude inside her boarding house. Elma Wells was also found naked and crammed into the closet of a vacant apartment that she had been showing. Every one of these murders matched up to Earle's usual pattern, yet there could be no certainty that he had actually committed them, and he showed no difference in his response to being accused of them to being accused of the murders that we know for a fact that he committed.

Mary Murray, Lena Weiner, and Ola McCoy were killed in Philadelphia, Pennsylvania, through November of 1925. All were strangled and raped after death, and items of men's clothing were stolen from most of the properties where they were discovered. Earle knew nothing about them. He'd never heard of them. He'd never heard of any of these women whom he was accused of killing. That he had been seen within the moments before their death. Of course, with no witnesses, there was no way to prove for certain that those six murders had been committed by Earle.

Finally, another desperate-looking detective from San Francisco arrived to try his luck. Isabel Gallegos had been murdered in August of 1926, and the police had arrested the man that they believed was her killer shortly afterwards. Russian immigrant John Slivkoff seemed like a perfect fit for the killing, but in line-ups, witnesses could not identify him, so he was cut loose. The trip up to see Earle Nelson was a cynical attempt to tie the crime to a serial murderer and clear it off the books. Earle denied it. Earle denied everything. To this day, it is still unclear which, if any, of these murders were the work of Earle Nelson. He was certainly in the right geographical area at the time to commit them, and he was clearly capable of committing them, yet insufficient evidence exists to connect him to them for certain.

When it became clear that he was not going to confess and save them all a lot of trouble, the police finally gave the press access to Earle. Everyone in the world wanted to hear what he had to say. All of the world was looking at him, desperate to know what was going on in his mind.

All of his dark deeds had been brought to light. All of his lies were exposed. There was no more need for hiding. No more need for shame. His face cracked into a smile and he said, 'I only do my lady killings on a Friday night.'

The reporters went wild. Earle's questionable charisma came to the fore, and he not only gave detailed confessions to his crimes, but he provided details too gruesome for the press to publish. He told them everything that they wanted to know and more, interspersing the prurient details of his necrophilia with quotations from Revelations, trying time and time again to explain to the world that he was on a holy mission.

The police finally managed to drag him away from his adoring public, wrote up a full confession containing everything that he had just said to the reporters, and presented it to him to sign. He refused. He recanted. He had done nothing wrong, and they couldn't prove that he had done anything wrong.

In June of 1927, Earle's trial was scheduled to begin, but his representative, James Stitt, requested a postponement. He claimed that the police's incompetent handling of the situation had made it impossible for his client to receive a fair trial. The papers were awash with blood, every detail of Earle's horrific crimes laid out in black and white. There was no way that a jury could be expected to try Earle based on the evidence presented when the police had allowed so much 'hearsay' into the court of public opinion. While Justice Dysart disagreed with the sentiment of the postponement, he could not argue with the truth of the matter, and a postponement was allowed until November, when the press coverage had begun to die down and there was at least the vague possibility of a jury being assembled who hadn't already decided that Earle was a monster.

Stitt continued to be an able and ardent defender of his client throughout the trial, making no attempts to deny the facts of the matter which were clear as day, but instead arguing for clemency on the basis that Earle Nelson was clearly mentally ill. A parade of doctors and specialists, including many who had treated him through the years, were brought forth to testify on his behalf. His Aunt Lillian took the stand to describe his behaviour through the years, not as if he were some hardened psychopath, but as though he were a child trapped in a man's body, one prone to the mood swings of a child and a child's foolishness.

An elderly woman who had employed Earle as a groundskeeper for a stint in 1926 and suffered no ill effect painted the saddest picture of Earle's childlike nature. He would talk to himself all day long, and she observed him stand outside in the pouring rain with no jacket on, just smiling up at the sensations that the sky was granting him.

Even his ex-wife, Mary Martin, came out of hiding to speak in his favour. She loathed the man for the way that he had treated her, but even so, she would not see him hanged. Not if her words could prevent it. She testified to his bizarre behaviour, the shifts in his moods, and even the vile sexual acts that he seemed compelled to commit. A litany of disgusting actions that probably did more to sour the jury against him than the factual statements of the police.

When the time came for a verdict to be handed down, it was as close to an open and shut case as the court had ever seen. There was barely a half-hour of deliberation before the twelve men of the jury came back with a unanimous guilty verdict. They did not care if he was mentally ill, they did not care if he heard the voices of angels telling him to kill. All that mattered to the jury was that the world would be a better place without Earle Nelson in it. On November 5, he was sentenced to death by hanging from the neck.

There was no possibility of appeal, and even the many letters that the court received after the fact from acquaintances of Earle willing to testify to his insanity, and medical experts with records of the same, could do nothing to change the situation. To the last moment, Earle was still lost in his mind, ranting and rambling to himself, trying to make peace with his God.

The God that had commanded him to commit the acts for which he had been accused, indicted, and damned still spoke to him, and he still whispered back his answers. Yes and no. Praise and damnation. Over and over, the guards would pause outside his cell and hear him repeating the same quote from the Book of Proverbs.

'My son, give me thine heart, and let thine eyes observe my ways. For a whore is a deep ditch; and a strange woman is a narrow pit. She also lieth in wait as for a prey, and increase the transgressors among men.'

This quotation, along with the innumerable psychiatric studies undertaken throughout those months, gives the modern reader the best opportunity to understand the logic behind Earle's actions.

He was almost the stereotype of the modern serial killer, a psychopath obsessed with his own pleasure, punishing women for 'leading him astray'. To the last, he would not accept any responsibility for his actions. To the last, he blamed the whole world for making him the way that he was. He blamed the same God he praised for all of his miseries. There was no contradiction in his mind between his image of himself as a pure and perfect Christian and the brutal murders that he had committed for his sexual gratification. He blamed his victims for tempting him rather than himself for giving in to that temptation.

He spent his last hours on earth quoting the entirety of the book of Revelations from memory. Finishing up just a few minutes before the hangman came.

On January 13, 1928, Earle was led out thirteen steps from Vaughn Street Gaol, then climbed up the gallows under his own steam. That was lucky for the wardens - they couldn't have carried a man that size up if he'd resisted. Looking out into the baying crowd, Earle's eyes gleamed.

The hangman cried out for silence so that the final words of the guilty could be heard. Earle threw back his head and brayed. 'I am innocent. I stand innocent before God and man. I forgive those who have wronged me and ask forgiveness of those I have injured. God have mercy!'

The noose was looped over his head and drawn up tight against his skin. This was the way that his victims had died, a cord around their necks, the air stolen from their lungs. But where Earle had been languorous in his torment, the law drew no pleasure in stringing out his demise. There was a short drop, then his weight snapped his neck.

Earle Nelson remained at the heart of a media frenzy for decades after his demise. Even as late as the forties, Alfred Hitchcock made a film based on Earle's story, called Shadow of a Doubt. To the general public, he was the first real 'superstar criminal' who everyone had heard of, and around whom whole conversations could revolve.

To criminologists, he was far more interesting. According to crime historians Everitt and Schechter, Earle Nelson was the first serial 'sex murderer' in the recorded history of the United States, and with over twenty confirmed victims, he remained the most prolific serial killer in history until fifty years later, when Dean Corll finally surpassed his body count.

The Gorilla Killer, the Dark Strangler, the Gorilla Man, Charles Harrison, Adrian Harris, Virgil Wilson, Earle Nelson, and Earle Leonard Ferral were all one man, and though he may have passed unseen through the world during his life, the mark that he left on the psyche of America can still be seen to this day.

Want More?

Did you enjoy *Gorilla Killer* and want some more True Crime?

YOUR FREE BOOK IS WAITING

From bestselling author Ryan Green

There is a man who is officially classed as "**Britain's most dangerous prisoner**"

The man's name is Robert Maudsley, and his crimes earned him the nickname "**Hannibal the Cannibal**"

This free book is an exploration of his story...

★★★★★ *"Ryan brings the horrifying details to life. I can't wait to read more by this author!"*

Get a free copy of **Robert Maudsley: Hannibal the Cannibal** when you sign up to join my Reader's Group.

www.ryangreenbooks.com/free-book

Every Review Helps

If you enjoyed the book and have a moment to spare, I would really appreciate a short review on Amazon. Your help in spreading the word is gratefully received and reviews make a huge difference to helping new readers find me. Without reviewers, us self-published authors would have a hard time!

Type in your link below to be taken straight to my book review page.

US	geni.us/gkUS
UK	geni.us/gkUK
Australia	geni.us/gkAUS
Canada	geni.us/gkCA

Thank you! I can't wait to read your thoughts.

About Ryan Green

Ryan Green is a true crime author who lives in Herefordshire, England with his wife, three children, and two dogs. Outside of writing and spending time with his family, Ryan enjoys walking, reading and windsurfing.

Ryan is fascinated with History, Psychology and True Crime. In 2015, he finally started researching and writing his own work and at the end of the year, he released his first book on Britain's most notorious serial killer, Harold Shipman.

He has since written several books on lesser-known subjects, and taken the unique approach of writing from the killer's perspective. He narrates some of the most chilling scenes you'll encounter in the True Crime genre.

You can sign up to Ryan's newsletter to receive a free book, updates, and the latest releases at:

WWW.RYANGREENBOOKS.COM

More Books by Ryan Green

In July 1965, teenagers Sylvia and Jenny Likens were left in the temporary care of Gertrude Baniszewski, a middle-aged single mother and her seven children.

The Baniszewski household was overrun with children. There were few rules and ample freedom. Sadly, the environment created a dangerous hierarchy of social Darwinism where the strong preyed on the weak.
What transpired in the following three months was both riveting and chilling. The case shocked the entire nation and would later be described as "The single worst crime perpetuated against an individual in Indiana's history".

More Books by Ryan Green

On 29th February 2000, John Price took out a restraining order against his girlfriend, Katherine Knight. Later that day, he told his co-workers that she had stabbed him and if he were ever to go missing, it was because Knight had killed him.

The next day, Price didn't show up for work.

A co-worker was sent to check on him. They found a bloody handprint by the front door and they immediately contacted the police. The local police force was not prepared for the chilling scene they were about to encounter. Price's body was found in a chair, legs crossed, with a bottle of lemonade under his arm. He'd been decapitated and skinned. The "skin-suit" was hanging from a meat hook in the living room and his head was found in the kitchen, in a pot of vegetables that was still warm. There were two plates on the dining table, each had the name of one of Price's children on it.

She was attempting to serve his body parts to his children.

More Books by Ryan Green

In 1902, at the age of 11, Carl Panzram broke into a neighbour's home and stole some apples, a pie, and a revolver. As a frequent troublemaker, the court decided to make an example of him and placed him into the care of the Minnesota State Reform School. During his two-year detention, Carl was repeatedly beaten, tortured, humiliated and raped by the school staff.

At 15-years old, Carl enlisted in the army by lying about his age but his career was short-lived. He was dishonourably discharged for stealing army supplies and was sent to military prison. The brutal prison system sculpted Carl into the man that he would remain for the rest of his life. He hated the whole of mankind and wanted revenge.

When Carl left prison in 1910, he set out to rob, burn, rape and kill as many people as he could, for as long as he could. His campaign of terror could finally begin and nothing could stand in his way.

More Books by Ryan Green

In 1861, the police of a rural French village tore their way into the woodside home of Martin Dumollard. Inside, they found chaos. Paths had been carved through mounds of bloodstained clothing, reaching as high as the ceiling in some places.

The officers assumed that the mysterious maid-robber had killed one woman but failed in his other attempts. Yet, it was becoming sickeningly clear that there was a vast gulf between the crimes they were aware of and the ones that had truly been committed.

Would Dumollard's wife expose his dark secret or was she inextricably linked to the atrocities? Whatever the circumstances, everyone was desperate to discover whether the bloody garments belonged to some of the 648 missing women.

Free True Crime Audiobook

Listen to four chilling True Crime stories in one collection. Follow the link below to download a FREE copy of *The Ryan Green True Crime Collection: Vol. 3.*

WWW.RYANGREENBOOKS.COM/FREE-AUDIOBOOK

"Ryan Green has produced another excellent book and belongs at the top with true crime writers such as M. William Phelps, Gregg Olsen and Ann Rule" –**B.S. Reid**

"Wow! Chilling, shocking and totally riveting! I'm not going to sleep well after listening to this but the narration was fantastic. Crazy story but highly recommend for any true crime lover!" –**Mandy**

"Torture Mom by Ryan Green left me pretty speechless. The fact that it's a true story is just...wow" –**JStep**

"Graphic, upsetting, but superbly read and written" –**Ray C**

WWW.RYANGREENBOOKS.COM/FREE-AUDIOBOOK

Made in the USA
Columbia, SC
16 May 2022